PRAISE

"*The Book of Assassinations* is a remarkable achievement, a book of *Illuminations*, full of odd turns and surprises; *Streets for Two Dancers* is a repository of unusual insights, moving observations and getting it absolutely right. Gibbons's is a very intriguing oeuvre."
—Marjorie Perloff, author *21st Century Modernism: The New Poets*

"[*Of D.C.*] is admirable, and astonishing. You are where Rimbaud was when he got to the *Illuminations*…What poets have preceded you in the D of C: Whitman, Pound, Olson!"
—Guy Davenport, author of *The Geography of Imagination*,
letter, June 4, 1992

"What especially impresses me about Gibbons's achievement in his writing is its rare synthesis. He is able to draw on an enormous breadth of knowledge and interdisciplinary reference, a sweeping vision…Remarkably, however, Robert manages to apprehend the most quotidian details of the life and flux around him, transfiguring such commonplace material into the hypnotic 'body' of his work."
—David Anfram, author of *Mark Rothko: The Works on Canvas*

"In his verse, Gibbons sees things others miss, extracting gains from the ruins of powerlessness in which the average citizen lives, offering then, a therapeutics for the public sphere."
—Jim Feast, *Evergreen Review*

"Robert Gibbons's new collection of poems lays bare the vast expanse of human history as a widening landscape of the most august imagination. Gibbons, a born maximalist, carries Charles Olson's excavations into the present tense, but does so in his own measure of music, personal and specific, yet universal and inclusive. *Animated Landscape* never forgets history is not a then, but always now, always all around us."
—Richard Deming, Director of Creative Writing, Yale University

UNDER THE GREAT DIVIDE
WITH ED DORN

UNDER THE GREAT DIVIDE WITH ED DORN
Copyright © 2024 by Robert Gibbons
ISBN: 978-1-960451-05-7
Library Of Congress Number:

First paperback edition published by Stalking Horse Press, May 2024

All rights reserved. Except for brief passages quoted for review or academic purposes, no part of this book may be reproduced, stored in a retrieval system, or transmitted by any means without the written permission of the author and publisher. Published in the United States by Stalking Horse Press.

www.stalkinghorsepress.com

Design by James Reich

Stalking Horse Press
Santa Fe, New Mexico

UNDER THE GREAT DIVIDE
WITH ED DORN

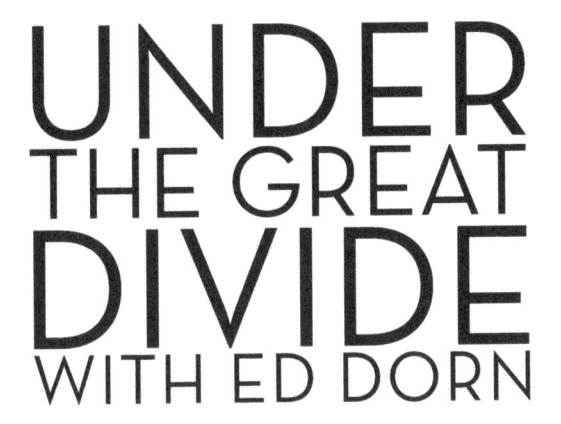

ROBERT GIBBONS

STALKING HORSE PRESS
SANTA FE, NEW MEXICO

CONTENTS

Prelude to Today - 13
We're Here Now - 14
The Torchlight - 15
At No Small Cost - 17
At the End of the Circuitous Route - 19
Colfax, in Fact - 21
After Sighting the Halo above the Woman - 23
The Woman in the Mountain - 25
This Is Also The West - 26
Under the Great Divide - 27
This Feminine Note - 28
Two Stultified Hands - 29
The Truer Vision - 30
The Woman in the Mountain II - 31
The Swallow at Red Rocks - 32
The Gift - 34
From Sunrise to Sundown to Walt's Crossing, March 7, '17 - 35
On a Photograph of Silver Ingots Piled High at Leadville - 36
Lone Ponderosa Pine - 38
Learning How to Drive - 39
Fenollosa, Who Calls Lightning a Sentence - 40
Golden, Colorado - 41
Long Lost Friends - 43
Song of the Fairly Useless, Hollow Gourd - 46
Only the Hot, Internal News - 48
Amalgamation of Saints - 49
Letters Written Across Both Earth & Sky - 51
The Newest Move - 52
Here's a Netherlandish Woodcut - 53
I want to Talk Abou You - 54
In Its Thrall - 55
Gaudier-Brzeska 10/4/91-6/5/15 -23 - 58
These Walls - 58
Mahler in Mind - 60
High Altitude Sonnet - 62

...CONTENTS

Marking the Indelible - 63
On the Perimeter - 64
In Lieu of Discerning - 67
Balance of Creation - 68
Just Sitting around, Listening - 69
Hear from None - 72
How Can a Man Trouble Himself toward Loneliness? - 73
Standing Silent at Ed Dorn's Grave - 74
As Men in Denver - 77
Believing They're the Real Thing - 79
As the Neon Moon Nears - 81
Doubts about How often One Word Can Stand Alone - 82
Lengthy Longevity of the Dream - 83
At This Elevation - 86
Straight to Boone - 87
Such Linguistic Imprints - 89
Now, Here, August 16th in Colorado - 90
Waxing to Waning - 91
Even Scratches Heard on Vinyl Are of Use - 92
Lessening the Everyday Heaviness - 94
Quiet Shoutout for a Longtime Friend - 96
Pulling into Granby - 97
To Make it Home - 98
Antares Stares Down - 100
Our Newest Path - 101
So Civil, the Seven of Them - 102
Italian Architect from Another Century - 103
Driving into the Day All the Way from the Night Before - 105
My Immediate Vision - 106
Leaping Cliff Ledge to Glacial Erratics - 107
Calligraphic Sign *Guang* - 109
What the Sun is Doing - 112
Her Rhythmic Tone - 113
Western Frontier Experiment - 114
Eclipse, Denver, December 13, 2016 - 115

...CONTENTS

Tonight: the Small but Distinctive Constellation, Corvus - 116
Raven - 117
Giving Birth to Another Day - 118
Monday - 120
At the Turn, Peering into Dorn's World - 121
Finding Venus Embedded Deep in Indigo - 122
Unknown - 124
Time, as Separate - 126
Crisscrossings - 128
Sun & Smoke - 129
Sign & Symbol - 130
That Was Then - 131
Our Memory Alone - 132
Blue Hands, Grey Jacket - 133
The Wind Sang - 134
Eleven Lines of Adoration - 135
Then Man Steps In - 136
Balance of Any Man or Woman - 137
Down the San Juan River on the Solstice - 138
You Have to Turn the Map Around - 140
Long Enough There to Get Here - 141
Against the Propensity - 143

The Irascible, Oracular Voice of Edward Dorn - 145

"Forever in America is about as long as it takes the sun to go down."
—Edward Dorn, *Real Towns Don't Have Parking Meters*

"Man came here by an intolerable way…He has, to begin again, one answer, one point of resistance only to such fragmentation, one organized ground, a ground he comes to by a way the precise contrary of the cross, of spirit in the old sense, in old mouths. It is his own physiology he is forced to arrive at."
—Charles Olson, *The Resistance*

"Man's response to ideas and things in the past must be learned. But they are not all. There are subtle means of communication that have been lost by mankind, as our nerve ends have been cauterized by schooling. The arts, especially the performing arts are more and more valuable in such restorations. For these nerves must be renewed, in both ourselves as faculty and in the students who come to us to communicate and to learn to communicate. To learn to move, at least without fear, to feel, see, touch also without fear, or at least without denials of first hungers, to be aware of everything around us (again, including especially people) - this is to start to penetrate the past and to feel as well as mentally see our way into the future."
—John A. Rice, Founder of Black Mountain College

"I watched you suffer a dull aching pain
Now you've decided to show me the same
No sweeping exit or offstage lines
Could make me feel bitter or treat you unkind
Wild horses couldn't drag me away"
—Keith Richards / Mick Jagger, *Wild Horses*

"To turn the threatening future into a fulfilled 'now,' the only telepathic miracle, is a work of bodily presence of mind."
—Walter Benjamin, *One-Way Street*

"Across this spectrum including the divine, the primitive, and the adolescent, what remains constant is a powerful erotic charge."
—Stephen Fredman, *The Contemporaries: A Reading of Charles Olson's, 'The Lordly and Isolate Satyrs'*

"…'earing the low chordes of the Foothills…"
—Edward Dorn, *The Winterbook*

In Memory of Ed, & for Jennifer Dunbar Dorn

PRELUDE TO TODAY

*When the crush of jagged, atonal
orchestral sounds
of the hundred car freight train dividing
the city
woke me up
from the depths
of the dream of fire & love,
I couldn't recall it
immediately,
lost
in the unconscious,
dropping further
out of sight.*

*It wasn't until I saw the image of the dancer
that she brought back to life
the depths of the dream
of fire & love,
so that the joy
of the rescue by the jagged, atonal
orchestral sounds
of the hundred car freight train dividing
the city,
coupled with the flight
of arms, legs, neck, head, & torso of the dancer,
became a prelude
to today.*

WE'RE HERE NOW

We're here now,
which every line
could begin with
as we traipse cross
country, but there
was that time
on I-80 West
with exits
to Marengo
& North English
just ahead, when
it made both
geographical & celestial
sense to see sunrise
in the rearview
as we sped
through Iowa
past nothing
on both sides
but trailer truck
convoys on the way
to Lincoln.
In jig time
Belle Plaine rose
up before us
with signs
to What Cheer
south & north
toward Waterloo
making us glad
& wary at once
to be in between
to be here there.

THE TORCHLIGHT

*The true modernism is not austerity
but a garbage strewn plenitude.* —Susan Sontag

Now he's scavenging wet detritus
he banged tore ripped pounded
hammered chiseled manhandled
diligently
without stop bludgeoned sawed drilled
crowbarred scratched out of green
ten-by-four-by-five dumpsters
from the apartment complex
across the way.

One of six on wheels he has to link together,
a good-sized train of trash
I saw just last week filled with
mattresses
& couches, broken chairs & tables
discarded
by end-of-the-month tenants moving
out & away
to what they
hope
is a better
place.

But this train today was the
usual garbage & trash barely recycled
in these parts, so that the thunderstorm
last night added a real burden to this guy's
already thankless task
with eight inches of rain
filling
the bottom of the swill.

. . .

After the big truck came
by
at the allotted time
unloading most
of the contents at least half the water
remained,
& this guy with reflector vest still on in
the swelter
of the sun, although smart to be under a carport,
couldn't let the water stand, stink, mold, infect,
singlehandedly tipping the heavy steel crate on its
side,

crawling inside to find just how many days'
months' years' worth of waste & what kind
of slime is stuck to the walls
of what I saw as a small cave
with him on his murky knees inside like a miner.
A hero.

Now he's welding a wheel back on
must have snapped, when singlehandedly tipping
the thing back upright. Lunchtime's been & gone
for him without a break or bite to eat. Saw him take
but a drink of water. Just hit
a dent in the inside wall
with sledgehammer again, now squats,
welding within the darkness of the
cavern.

The Torchlight may not be as
monumental as Liberty, but as
he finishes the fourth car of the
train, two remain, the power of
the monumental is merely the
equal
here to the humility of the
anonymous.

AT NO SMALL COST

Seven days into the new year
             winter's worth
of snow
piled high
on Sunday
morning enough
to offer Peace for
the short term, Hope
against inevitable February
doldrums.

Not surprising I don't go
out in it, but stay put
inside
inside this
currently affordable
apartment with all utilities
& find myself
parallel

to Weir Gulch
banked by prairie
grass & cottonwoods
on another good day
same time last year,
where this body
of water ran
from Lakewood,
where I found myself
so often, through working-
class sections of west Denver
including Westwood, Barnum,
Villa Park, & Sun Valley.

                                               …

Weir Gulch, where cutthroat
brown & rainbow trout still run,
& one can sense where natives
harnessed makeshift twine
& wood fish gear (weir),
after which later
settlers took over,
at no small cost
to either faction,
& renamed
the stream
in English.

AT THE END OF THE CIRCUITOUS ROUTE

In one strip mall on Colfax Avenue there
are two dollar
stores, Tree & Family.

In the first one you can buy a quarter
frozen chicken so many who could use it don't
have an oven.

Giant orange, green, & brown bottles of soda.
Crepe paper for decorating, if & when
son or daughter can't find

a job return,
or not,
from wars beyond Iraq or Afghanistan.

Lines are long at Dollar Tree.
On this occasion Christmas
decorations prominent:

stars, balls, Santa hats,
nothing religious,
no crèche,

Wisemen with frankincense,
no donkey, nor
menorah, Hanukkah absent.

She got some batteries for kids' toys.
I found two fine, lined notebooks,
both of course, imported from China.

...

We eyed Family Tree five doors down
past Planet Fitness from where we stood
at H&R Block. Instead, minutes later, before

our daily walk around the lakes behind the library,
I caught sight of the woman living out of her car,
clothes & clothes baskets, plastic bottle

of bleach on the library parking lot space
next to her house trying to tidy up. I'm afraid
I had the gall to go on over, after taking

a double sawbuck out of my wallet, "Hi"
"Hi," immediately turning & going on about
her business. "Don't be offended, but could you

use this?" She stared down at the black-gloved
hand, which if it held a dollar I knew she would
have refused, if not spat. Took it with a humble nod

of gratitude. Joined my wife on the walk thinking
both about the woman & our own future at the same time.
At the end of the circuitous route she asked how old in my

estimation the woman in the car for a home was?
I'm afraid I remained silent, sensing what she thought I might say.
"Around my age?" "I'm not going to say THAT."

We drove home, thankful, knowing that
by my getting behind the wheel, & her climbing
into the passenger seat we weren't already there.

COLFAX, IN FACT

You can't put anything past Colfax Avenue,
I mean anything,
I mean anything can happen,
or appear out of the ordinary on Colfax, so when
we stopped in at Big Bunny Motel
with all our fears,
jobless, no trust fund
like most of the kids the day before
yesterday waiting in line for brunch,
not out of mere curiosity,
but just to get some water out of the cooler in the trunk, innocent
ex-cons cautious of each other
as need be, either approaching,
or avoiding, & housekeeper carrying a whole roomful
of dirty bedding,
that other world that's downright real,
& more upright than those checking bank statements, or
the fourteen-year-old we saw
off skateboard only
to stick his own card in ATM, wheel
on down the sidewalk, no, the halo over the head
of the Little Person in front
of me at the Colfax Safeway took
a doubletake took a doubletake
at my grocery cart with Evian
& full case of *Arrowhead*
Mountain spring, she's
agog, because she's
got one item only,
one sole item
only: Coke
Bottling's
Dasani

...

purified water, which contains magnesium sulfate & potassium chloride
& table salt added to municipal water sources, renamed *Aquarius* in Brazil,
Ciel in Mexico, & advertised as *Spunk* in
London.

I felt guilty as Hell.
Especially when I watched
her have to pay more for that
single bottle of impure liquid
than I was going to have to pay
for a case of local spring. Granted,
I'd wanted to intervene even before
then, wanting to offer her water from
my case for free, but didn't have the guts
to interfere with laissez-faire commerce, nor
risk her ire that I would do so because she was
a Little Person about my wife's age on the street,
Colfax, in fact, with her invisible innocent halo only
I could see.

AFTER SIGHTING THE HALO ABOVE THE WOMAN

So next day,
after sighting the halo above
the woman in line ahead of me at Colfax Safeway,
we're back in Boulder
after picking up bread & green beans at the farmer's market
sitting in folding canvas chairs
on the sidewalk
in front of our parked car on 14th between Spruce & Pine Streets
across from Lucile's,
where the monied stand outside in the brunchline
we refuse to,
asking only for 2 cups to go,
which cost six bucks
as it is.

We're sitting there
in the shade of a black locust sipping
coffee & munching on Izzio's seven grain,
when my wife says a carload of
(I can't hear her because she's keeping her voice down
& I'm hard of hearing
as it is, a carload of what, Honey,
Africans, I ask
half-facetiously would be 100%
exception to white rule here on 14th between Spruce & Pine,
no. Native Americans? No. Who, then?)
Whispers: Little People.

I breathe this heavenly sigh of celestial validation
because I saw the Saint with halo yesterday,
& here, back of me are a bunch of miraculous acolytes assembled
first around the meter the mother
struggles to pay for with her cell phone,
while a teenage couple go hand-in-hand toward the market,

the father walks
the dog & two younger daughters a few trees down
to wait in the shade for the fee to be paid,
manifesting 14th Street
between Spruce & Pine halos
only my wife can see.

THE WOMAN IN THE MOUNTAIN

She saw the Woman in the Mountain first
telling me of two breast peaks the others
nose lips chin forehead belly knee
& feet, so I looked & watched
her stand & walk away
straight ahead into
clouds above.

THIS IS ALSO THE WEST

Go from Cody Street, granted
before the crosswalk at Carr Street
traffic light on 20th, letting white sedan
ease past with window open on a day when
AC should be on, but he don't like you jaywalking
so close behind his vehicle, even if it's 15 meters away
staring hard in his rearview at your blackthorn shillelagh
he surely can't quite grasp the meaning of, stops at red light
glaring at you, but at the same time making damnwell sure you
read white letters on rear windshield: Protected by: .45 cacp,
which in my far from tenderfoot Eastern lingo equals, **45 caliber automatic
Colt pistol**, so trudge on in extra heavy boots taking his disdain to heart
knowing full-well I'm in my element in my territory following wife
walking daughter's dog for the full purpose of protecting her, if
not dog with this Irish blackthorn shillelagh turning Western
heads heading toward Morse Park's bower of incredibly
old shagbark hickory, which steel-tipped blackthorn
seems to divine, & in camaraderie with the trees
quickly sidles up next to each of them.

UNDER THE GREAT DIVIDE

It was eerie crawling
train wheels navigating
under the Great Divide, while
my mind sensed a dead reckoning
connection north to the Bering Strait, south
down to where I earlier alluded to her
to Oaxaca & Chiapas through the Andes
with that photograph of David's Intihuatana or
Hitching Post to the Sun at both Equinoxes,
(which I thanked him for, again, just this week
close to forty years after it was taken)
both Bolivia & Chile all the way
down to Argentina's Patagonia
& Tierra del Fuego.

We weren't far from the highest point
of the US Divide at Grays Peak.

With Glenwood Canyon our immediate destination,
my imagination lifted out of that tunnel past Sorensen & Winter Park
toward the Alps, Munich, & Salzburg, Rijeka,
Split, & Belgrade
fifty years ago come summer,
& forward waking up in the room
at Hotel Colorado to dark rain & potential
disappointment for the day
planned ahead, when all of a sudden
she asked if that weren't the Sun climbing the mountain,
spectrum Sun caused
beginning as a simple pillar
built at the foot of the hill into a higher arc
as if offering an embrace between two peaks, this sign convincing us
of our destiny.

THIS FEMININE NOTE

She saw that
photo of me standing
in front of the monumental
outcrop phallic reach
of it all ascending into sun-bleached sky,
while I claimed
to intuit Precambrian
granite below alluvial
washed sandstone,
all she could
comment
on was the more immediate
evidence & color of red & pink
grains of feldspar
on the path
below boot soles
underfoot.

This feminine note
continues to ground me
in space & time more closely
than depth of unseen
granite, or height
of monument's reach.

TWO STULTIFIED HANDS

Top window light concentrating in diagonal lines & rays
mid-wall to floor, flowing bent against
the old steamer trunk standing
vertically in the corner
once belonged
to Mr. & Mrs. Albert Kreglinger of 9 Grand Place,
Antwerp, now holds
the Bose playing Coltrane's,
"Then I'll Be Tired of You," which case can't be
true with me for you,
reminding me here by its simple
rhythm alone,
my father,
who came from a family
of vaudevillians,
tried his damnedest to teach me
even the most elemental notes
of *Tea for Two*, but fingers
wouldn't but budge, knot,
plunge making his eyes
roll up inside his skull
in full visceral
exasperation,
wondering
what the
Hell I was
ever going to
do with myself
& these ten fingers
on two stultified hands.

THE TRUER VISION

One of those grand misprisions this
time on a Black Man's washboard
abdomen, Tupac Shakur's
tattoo photographed
by rockstar insider,
Danny Clinch,
& all I saw of the image,
as positioned, *Hug Life*, &
dug it the most as some kind
of posthumous message from the grave,

just as the lone lonely letter "T" came
slowly out of its oblique angle
into the truer vision of *Thug
Life*. But *Hug Life*
continued to
resonate
with me
& both
Hug & *Thug*
merged into their
rime, complicity, & nearness
to the simplicity of any skin's intimacy.

THE WOMAN IN THE MOUNTAIN II

There's that note
still ringing in my ear
McCoy Tyner makes, so
singly, shortly into "Goodbye."

My recently chiseled
face with worries
over daughter's
circum/stances.

Chicken soup for breakfast, this
poet's economy hovering just above
expanding abyss of poverty, his chiseled
face with worries over daughter's circum/stances.

Woman in the Mountain within listening distance
offers much needed solace, however silent her
words. Woman in the Mountain, I tramp
& Braille, as if she were a written text.

THE SWALLOW AT RED ROCKS

Just back from the Fountain Formation, once part
of what geologists call the Ancestral Rockies
formed 300 million years ago, intrigued me
no end, & to tears, really,
when I asked the Native American guide
which trail to take, & that three weeks ago we
were in Maine.

She warmed up
to name the one she favored
with her own visceral affection showing
in that brilliant, aboriginal
visage.

The night before at the party little Lily told me
her mother was a geologist.
Went straight up to the living room where she sat
with our two daughters drinking some
rum or tequila concoction, all three offering
me some from weird plastic cups
with bent straws,
which I declined.

Talked to Kristen,
Lily's mother, of both girls on either side of her there,
& that their Great-grandfather
on their mother's side,
L. Don Leet,
was Head of the Geology Department
at Harvard, & in 1948 published a book titled,
Causes of Catastrophe: Earthquakes, Volcanoes, Tidal Waves, & Hurricanes,
& that she could be part of this Western Vision Quest
I'm on helping identify the stones
I seek here as I had back home in Portland & Gloucester

like the Sandstone Man my digging
bar hit while trying to help Kathleen plant flowers
for her father, sister, & niece.

Sandstone Man smiling even
with the arrowhead wedged
in the back of his head.

Back at Red Rocks Park next day,
after all night partying, when Kristen promised
to help identify the geology here
in the West,
I could feel the Precambrian granite lodged
under later sandstone
& feldspar.

Tears that welled up when asking
the Native American guide which trail to take had dried up
like long-gone streams helped
carve these monuments.
All along the two-mile trail with signs marked as Difficult
sandstone smiled
down.

The swallow that seemed to follow us
volunteered to be
our vision quest image,
what with her translucent wings
we still could see through to the sky.

THE GIFT

When the swallow lifts her
gold breast & belly in surprise
just a few feet from one's eyes…

FROM SUNRISE TO SUNDOWN TO WALT'S CROSSING, MARCH 7, '17

Sundown steady blazing
crack of light between Foothills near
& formidable, snow-laden Rockies beyond.
While sunrise earlier, opposite, presaged
a day we're headed out of here,
not without some minor regret
of leaving behind all
we've experienced.

No, we'll take that with us.
While in the long interim sharing
observations sparkling into our eyes
& those of Walt Whitman as he crossed
the East River on the Brooklyn Ferry
seems such a short time ago, marks
this moment in his words
eternal…

ON A PHOTOGRAPH OF SILVER INGOTS
PILED HIGH AT LEADVILLE

It's still rough
& tumble here
in Colorado where
one can leap
back in stages
of violent history:
Glenwood Springs'
early skirmishes
& false promises
used to clear Utes
from the territory;
or a bit further
into the future
where Irish miners
made millionaires
in silver at Leadville
of Boettchers, Browns,
Campions, Guggenheims
and Tabors, while making
$2.50—$3.00 for a ten-hour
dangerous day themselves.

When they went on strike
in 1896 at the Emmett Mine
to try & make a living wage,
then Governor McIntire
sent in the Guard, 653
to be exact broke
the strike, their will,
radical philosophy,
& back of the Union
itself, part of what
is termed Colorado Labor
Wars still seems to reverberate

here in hum & racket
of cars on the roads,
in unabashed rough
& tumble tones
of voice & chatter
in the bars, in all
the deafening cheers
for the local team.

LONE PONDEROSA PINE

Of course, it's a poor site,
this lone ponderosa pine
is rooted in above a creek
on Redfeather Rustic Road.
Near 500 years old at an elevation
over 8,000 feet in the abandoned
town site of Manhattan, Colorado.[*]

As the story goes 130 years ago word
got round about gold in the hills west
of Fort Collins. Local businessmen hired
three prospectors, who no sooner
confirmed the rumors than a rush
of 300 claims were filed.

Forty buildings sprung up: post office,
newspaper, casino, one room schoolhouse,
& mill to grind ore serving mining properties
named Bullfrog, Joker, Bacon, Laugh-a-Lot,
Wedding Bells, Honeymoon, & Evening Star.
By the turn of the twentieth century everyone
was gone.

Thirty years later what cabins remained
were torched by the Forest Service.

Of course, it's a poor site, this lone ponderosa pine
is rooted in
what with one local historian quoted saying that
every square foot
of the mountains within the boundaries south & north
from the foothills to the summit of Medicine Bow Range
 had been trod upon
in search of precious metals.

---

[*] Credit to Laurie Stroh Huckaby, et al, *Field Guide to Old Ponderosa Pines in the Colorado Front Range*, which led to Kenneth Jessen's, *Manhattan: Pourdre Canyon's Ghost Town*.

LEARNING HOW TO DRIVE

    Here I am in a Colorado basement
(Freud's floor) apartment wrapped in three blankets
    wearing socks
    & a Buffalo plaid,
    yesterday at exactly 3:00 in the afternoon
    on the way to Boulder
    the digital temp on the billboard read 100.

    She's in the other room working
(coughing) at the Yale library table
    wrapped in the Mexican blanket from Chiapas.
    Ed Dorn's brandishing
    his wry smile from the cover
    of a book Seth discounted
    for me at Red Letter
    along with the ever-present
    cigarette & beer.

We're here
   four hours
short of two weeks
               hear from no one
back East anymore,
          which suits me
learning how to drive
like an angry cowboy at my age is
essential to getting around
these crowded highways
     anger aplenty
        to harness,
bridle.

FENOLLOSA, WHO CALLS LIGHTNING A SENTENCE

Lightning strikes above the mountains out
of the dark storm sweeping across
them ridge-by-ridge southeast
writing in calligraphic strokes
sending me straight to Fenollosa,
who calls lightning a sentence.
Look at that: to place earth
over one's own image,
or to put evil away
equals self-effacement.

Fenollosa would see these
riderless horses crossing
through dark clouds.
Now this hint
of blue,
where the Woman
in the Mountain
looks bravely
up, swallows
cast a spell.

GOLDEN, COLORADO

Get out here, you're struck by space.
Just off the plane, mountains & clouds equal
a married couple, genders obvious & pure.
I know Colfax Ave. from previous visits to Denver.
Right now I'm at the beginning end of the road
in Golden, Colorado,
where the street began as Native American trading route,
becoming Heritage Road,
then Colfax, & I-40.
When I lifted the shades
of the hotel room window this morning
to this classic American plateau
almost near at hand,
all I could imagine were first peoples
standing at the edge
overlooking the vast plain
north. Forget that clichéd
image of men on horseback,
these were on foot, trekking,
migrating, wandering, totally inside
the space I said now strikes us.
They were part of it. Internalized it?
That's in the near distance, but right here
practically knocking on the window,
(& would tap perhaps if there were the slightest wind against it)
the first lodgepole pine I've ever seen.
It's strange & handsome at the same time.
I imagine hands in the pine-needled
branches to this tree without limbs,
if you can fathom that?
No, no limbs to the lodgepole pine,
so it became standard materiel for shelter
uses of the tipi. This is no history
lesson, however.

...

41

It's just that signs
like mountains & clouds
are forever turning up to validate
a writer's quest, then new ones like the first real plateau
one's seen, along with first lodgepole pine.

Yesterday, in the first hours on the ground here,
getting off at exit 262A from I-70 West,
there at the bottom juncture
straddling Colfax Ave.
at Golden,
a bearded guy
about thirty,
kind of smiling,
I don't know if he was busking,
or merely panhandling, when we took the corner
too fast to make out the difference, but I know he knew
what he was doing, when he wrote on the piece of cardboard
in large letters **ON THE ROAD**, & lower, **_need provisions_**.

No hobo, clothes too clean.
Maybe today's performance artist,
taking bus out here from Denver, who,
if we tossed him a dollar, we might overhear,
Go moan for man.

LONG LOST FRIENDS

Did not, no, want to waste
robin's egg
blue Ritz-Carlton stationery
on a poem,
saving it for preferred
letter
to a friend back home
the back home that may well
never be again
as I'd just about had it
with the Atlantic
    lobsters molting ahead of time
in warmer waters.

The lack
of anymore
than one friend, as Thoreau told it, she's the only
home I know now
that back way to say against
fully-clothed whispers
in the dark
she lights up
the Way
new batteries in both
flashlights,
while I Braille
on the flesh equal
to letters drawn across the beige
stationery
whisper words here
in the Foothills
of Colorado with these new
old stones talking
to me well

                                                            ...

in tongues
believe me the clouds are more solid
here & clear
heat manageable
paint drying on the house
while I sip the wine
redder than ever
cheaper, too, less than four bucks
meaning I'll never be poor
even without any work other
than scratching felt-tip
against beige Ritz-Carlton stationery
out of McLean, VA, where we also made
our escape from more than once,
ecstatically,
happy
to leave dull
corporate bosses
& yes-men
well & good & far behind.
Bloomsday yesterday made
Molly of her.
I barely left
the house, the basement,
Freud's favorite floor, & now my own,
after eight long days on the road,
where there was nothing
to pass, but Time
& trailer trucks,
& roadside sex
at night is
the tightly
guarded
secret of the road
road sex lighting up
the night, & lengthening the joy
of the journey, the secret
so well kept

& let out,
whispered
here
at the foothills.

I listen to the new
old stones become
my long lost friends.

SONG OF THE FAIRLY USELESS, HOLLOW GOURD

Woman at Lakewood Farmers Market
on Alameda Avenue, not far
from where Kerouac bought that cottage
with the $1,000 advance
from ***The Town & the City***,
painted a fairly useless, hollow
gourd Granny Smith green, adding
plastic leaf in order
to mimic giant apple.

Three weeks running, still there,
I had to ask how much?
"$12," so bought it, the fairly useless,
hollow gourd
now draws my eye toward it
as a work of folk art
before looking out past it
at the Woman in the Mountain
of the Foothills, or due South, Pikes
just West of Colorado Springs.

That shack is 1.3 miles from our new digs.
Kerouac with saintly ability to withstand poverty,
in fact, juxtaposing it to prosperity offered up
from New York, Harcourt Brace Editor, Bob Giroux,
whom he's just seen off at Denver Airport,
then walks & hitchhikes back to Denver, unproper: 27th & Welton,
where he surmises that ecstasies proffered up
from Giroux's White World are not
enough for him as he desires

to shed his skin
& become a Mexican
or African American in order
to experience their kicks, highs, jazz, girls, & *nights*.

Of course, as a poet, Jack is already transformed
into what Rimbaud & Akhmatova respectively said all poets are
= "niggers" & "yids" = experiencing an epiphany
under floodlights of all things of a neighborhood softball game,
where his Pride at trying to rise above local anonymity
in Lowell is revealed to him,
& where he says he dies
in Denver…

Then catches the trolley at the corner of Colfax & Broadway
to as close to his new digs as that transport will take him,
walking pitch-black Alameda back to the shack
at 6100 Center Avenue in the Westwood section,
where he'll reside for a mere two months before
heading out to San Francisco, if not a new man,
then man renewed.

The fairly useless, hollow gourd found
at the farmers market
just absorbed this reverie
in its entirety,
& will play it back,
if I ask,
percussive instrument
of memory & language
it has become balanced
on the windowsill
between the Woman in the Mountain
of the Foothills, Colorado Springs, & Pikes
just West beyond,
& me.

ONLY THE HOT, INTERNAL NEWS

My new method
is a matter of pacing,
not necessarily walking
as before evidenced
in the long piece written
in seven months
over three hundred fifty pages,
Anatomy & Geography, no,
now that there's more risk
involved knowing no one
out here just a few blocks
from all the danger visible
day & night in homeless
eyes & windows
of abandoned
buildings
on Colfax Avenue, I pace,
& rather than
following the plan
outlined
earlier overhearing
what the Solar Plexus had to say,
I'm interpreting only
what the hot,
internal news
gonads offer
up today.

AMALGAMATION OF SAINTS

Naked weather girl let us all know
        snow fell
        with three days left in August
onto Pikes looming large right
out the window here,
so the mountain beckoned us
all the way from there everyday
till a week before Autumn Equinox
yesterday 8:21 a.m.

We caught it there in the distance,
        but wanting a closer look mapped out
        old town Colorado Springs,
although by the time
we saw it from across
West Colorado Avenue
the red granite at fourteen
thousand feet
was bare.

Equinox, come & gone,
        spent sun's exact moment
        traversing EARTH'S center line
waiting in the dingy, dank, faceless
Department of Motor Vehicles.
Yes, dark morning a block
from the corner of Colfax & Wadsworth,
where the shaggy young man stands with cardboard sign:
TOO UGLY TO PROSTITUTE.

Instead, today, FREE,
        from the heavy-handed claws
        of bureaucracy & the law,
we'll spend this other holy day, if also somewhat awkwardly,

celebrating Coltrane's birthday
waiting for Duke Ellington to come over
KCSM Radio out of San Mateo & San Francisco
(that amalgamation of Saints like stones walked among
in the so-called Garden of the Gods) on *Take the Coltrane*.

LETTERS WRITTEN ACROSS BOTH EARTH & SKY

Canada geese scribbling vowels across the sky,
little garter snake
               consonants across our path
through this Western field filled
                   with prairie grass.

Now, coffee, felt-tip pen, both black,
           in contrast
       to mid-winter sun's blaze.
A girl in black tights,
             hair in long braid, armless

black top, sprints across the parking lot to finish
          off her jog.
Just as bright before my eyes as this
        mid-winter blaze,
               or letters written across both earth & sky.

THE NEWEST MOVE

That, just then,
the newest
balletic, or jazz,
almost unnatural,
but most natural move
in the air
right here, those two swallows
corkscrewing, as opposed to
dovetailing
their way away,
straight, although far
from that simple
delineation,
spiraling together wing-
to-wing
Southwest
in the direction
of the black
locust
just across
the way.

HERE'S A NETHERLANDISH WOODCUT

Here's a Netherlandish woodcut cut exactly
400 years before I was born in 1946
titled, *The Field has Eyes, the Wood Ears*,
which stood in for what I wanted
to say trekking Red Rocks, Evergreen,
Lookout Mountain here in our new
daily exploratory world West.

The figure of the man now
there in Berlin wearing red cloak mimicking
my own Buffalo plaid
covers his lips
with fingertips
seeming to know
he has nothing

to add to eyes
open on the ground
ears listening on each limb
of the trees during his
otherwise solitary,
gauntlet.

I WANT TO TALK ABOUT YOU

Skies darken over Colfax Ave.
homeless seek shelter
in doorways at Safeway, every
Pawn & Payday Loan storefront, even
Fillmore Auditorium, where
Dylan & Snoop Dogg performed,
while we abandon
umbrella *leitmotif* over a number
of screaming figures
by Francis Bacon,
walking the gauntlet past all the homeless
smoking in camaraderie,
& get home grateful just in time to hear
Coltrane blow on "I Want to Talk about You",
which is exactly
what I wanted to do all along here,
how you've made your way through nine states
to get here,
wear the same clothes
reaching back decades on the same
body I knew initially, evincing a courage
& patience unmatched,
inviolable,
which word Guy Davenport once applied
to the character of some painter,
or writer,
saint.

IN ITS THRALL

Here I be
reading, focused
on learning more, if
there's any room
for more, so
filled already with this
West, the words in front of me
run along fast & register, but during
the entire sojourn,
excursion along
letters sentences paragraphs pages,
the peripheral intervenes
& that dancing tree
shimmering out
the window
holding onto & shedding
leaves at the same time
is no stray.

Merely holds me in its thrall.
Not unlike the other day
when at the library,
where I'd chosen
the most remote
position away
from other patrons
the young woman chose
the table most immediately,
imminent,
in front
of me,
& turned with a smile before she sat down,
only to reveal the entire broad backless cinch of no idea
what she had on, began

                                                                                 …

to extend her arms
out from the rest
of the backless
cinch of undress
in rhythmic Indonesian
reach, where one hand's
fingers danced
upon the palm
of the other,
while she seemed to read this
choreography from a homemade
manuscript set down on said
table before her.

While seriously, I tried to focus
on my own task at hand
before me reading
just as I had been here,
while the tree danced right
out there in peripheral vision,
my discipline kicking in, but waffling
now & again
between the Indonesian
rhythm shared & expressed
silently in dance,
while silver miners
back there in Leadville, Colorado
either down the shaft in danger,
or worse, on strike in danger
against the owners, or law
enforcement protectors
from the state.

Who's to say?
I'm here right now
above the floor I slept on
that same night, when Hunter Moon
enveloped earth & me with light,

windows open to an air I'd
never known before.

It's as if, as I began
to say, this tree dancing
with leaves held onto, others
shed, partnered with the memory
of the woman, immediately imminent
instructing me at this ripe age to value
equally the known with that never known
before.

GAUDIER-BRZESKA 10/4/91—6/5/15-23

First night in the new place
with view of Rockies in the near
distance. She immediately says
she wants to take from them,
"absorb" their energy
which of course
tossed me
backward
& forward
at the same time toward
Pound's **VORTEX** begun
with Sculptural energy is the mountain.

She sees them, again, as mammaries
to abstract & suck from
rejuvenate herself
after the ordeal
of cross-country trek +
three weeks spent
in basement (Freud's floor)
apartment.

Upward our vision-quest images
swirled & zagged tens
of swallows radaring
avoidance at & away
from each other
in the high air
of Denver's
outskirts
writing
our Western
aliases on the Magic
Writing Pad of twilight.

THESE WALLS

These walls,
        how I love these
        protective walls, uterine

I imagine the valves of the heart
        opposing them, these,
                with twenty-foot ceilings,

to the plight of the homeless
        crossing with all their belongings
                Colfax Avenue infamous Colfax, longest,

wickedest street in America I cross every day
        in my car, not on holy sole of foot, offering up
                a nod of grace toward them, grateful for these

protective walls, the uterine,
        valves of the heart, opposing
                them with empathy to those

others' plight.

MAHLER IN MIND

Short day out here with Denver sunrise
at 7:10, set by 5:16 trying to manage
as much as possible in between,
what with revolt ongoing
around airports all over
the country: JFK, Logan, LAX, Sea-Tac,
where governor Inslee will call out the author
of the executive order as cruel & lacking in compassion,
& Virginia Governor McAuliffe at Dulles saying,
"Discriminatory tactics breed hatred,"
while at Dallas/Fort Worth International
crowds call for release
of those detained
illegally
Brooklyn Federal Court agrees.

Tear ourselves away from this America,
head over to Cody St. & wait for buyers
of crib our daughter placed on Craig's list.
Warm outside in driveway's Southwest sun
just before midday between sunrise & sundown
skin in contact with each minute ticking down
toward arrival of Gracie & Ricardo, their infant
supine in truck cab.

Help him load crib & boxspring
while Kathleen gathers up spare mattress
Gracie wants inside the house, Mahler in mind,
his marginal aesthetic saying composition is made from
the bottom up, which evidence I'll have pleasure of
rediscovering later in the afternoon
with headphones on
on Dietrich Fischer-Dieskau's version
of *Songs of a Wayfarer*, not far in tone & language
from that which would rise

ever so spontaneously out the diaphragm,
throat & tongue of my friend
Robert Hellman in Rockport
or Cambridge, took off

that long day
in 1973 from Nixon's America in order to exile
himself & family: wife Margaret, son J.B., & baby daughter
Miranda squatting in the Nørrebro District of København,
welcomed there by the Danes,
his voice resonating
within me as sundown
goes down quietly behind
these foothills, its light landing
somewhere West far beyond,
clouds charcoal grey
to silver, red, new
crescent moon
& Venus
suddenly out
of darkness out there now,
as if from the bottom up.

HIGH ALTITUDE SONNET

Polaris has me
      standing upright
           during what we call
the quiet hour between
      three & four in the morning,
           staring due North above foothills
of the Rockies,
      which have talked
           to us day & night, now
sleeping like her
      there in the room
           she still feels stranger in,
while I do my best
      as amateur astronomer
           to convince her that stars
are aligned here for us,
      & that although fear streams
           by now & again with high altitude winds,
the walls & windows
      of that room she's dreaming in will
           prevent all danger from coming in.

MARKING THE INDELIBLE

You get at it, more or less, late at night.
Words on the page. But then past all that,
texture of paper inviting print,
that weave, underlying
each letter subtle
impression
carrying lines along
into one's recognition
of words: star water plum
constellation handprint stone
wall dead stump leaves of mist,
it's as if one becomes transported
a number of millennia, not just back,
but forward, marking that which is indelible.

ON THE PERIMETER

Surely, we wouldn't have chosen this
particular place,
but Global Positioning led us
to the airport past all the chaos
a single accident can cause
on any major U.S. Highway I-70,
& I took note
of a town on the perimeter
to return to after dropping off
our passengers, hoping rush hour
back into Denver
would subside down
to its normal manic bronco-
bustin', calf-ropin', steer-ridin',
rodeo-antic, cattle-drivin', tail-gaitin'
Self.

Quietly, meandering back
toward that town with its anti-western
name of Brighton.
Brighton, no less.
Last name of an old flame
back in the Seventies in Jamaica Plain,
scooped up out
of Lesley College,
beaches outside New York
& London, this town tries
to hold on to those ties
with Hughes Station
& Penny Lane,
but a walk the entire length
of Main Street, South to North,
will reveal what culture rules
here with all
its body shops,

Valenzuela's,
beauty & nail shops,
the bars & bars
on windows,
& back again.

North to South,
where at 270 North Main the house shouts
BEWARE of DOG
on the chain-link gate
with no evidence of said
animal on the premises.

It's difficult to cross either
North to South
or South to North across East Bridge Street running straight through town
harshly bisecting Main
with unforgiving
eighteen-wheelers barrel-assing right off
US 85-N, but when we did
the 1886 one-room church vied
for our attention with the cherry-red
Corvette parked outside,
latter catching her
eye, the former
welding mine to the sole cobalt-blue
stained-glass window.

Next the tracks at the furthest end
South a spot two locals recommended,
where we sampled pinto beans,
huevos rancheros, & potatoes.
It was good.
Especially the green chili
served up with chips for free
before we ordered,
but once one's been to Mexico City,

Guadalajara, Oaxaca, Veracruz,
Cosamaloapan, Zihuatanejo,
nothing
Brighton's going
to serve up
is genuine Mexican,
other than
the Soul
& kindness
of its inhabitants.

IN LIEU OF DISCERNING

Years spent near
      the ocean, waves their say,
          now we wake to the sound
of mountains calling across great distances,
      watch swallows carry primordial messages,
         write lines in flight.

One
  wants all
    these correspondences
                out here
            in lieu of discerning
the murmur of a sole
           human voice.

BALANCE OF CREATION

Catch moonset, still
full, big round stone lit
up balancing above snowcapped,
jagged Rockies due West, not long after
sunrise, just opposite.

Our purely New England
genes are back there in time
& distance with all those as snow
falls wanting merely to curl up next
the fire to simply watch & listen.

Instead, we'll find small compensation
heading out into the 70-degree air, where
the Great Blue Heron swoops once out over
the lake away from the nest & returns strategically
behind the other to mount & mate.

JUST SITTING AROUND, LISTENING

Music is bad enough without
overhearing here outside at Baker Street Grill
with stout for me, brown ale for her,
this guy under the black locust
opposite us on the cell
rivaling the Muzak for
cacophony,

so I read outloud
Kerouac's **Sketches** about
finding some clothes on a dump,
which he's wearing, & inside the bag found
on a Pajaro levee dump, no less,
west of Watsonville,
& not as huge as the one
the train revealed on the way
from Guadalajara to Mexico City

— Nixon resigned forty-two years ago yesterday,
when I read
the headlines
in Spanish over
the shoulder of a cop sitting
in his cruiser in Mexico City &
we both gave each other a thumbs-up
in relief of a president's abdication,

& sure enough the guy I read Kerouac aloud over
his rivaling the cacophony
of the Muzak runs out
of others to call on the phone
who'll listen, leaves
me to his opposite, those sitting next to us
outside at the bar,

where in the Freedom
of our unemployed
irrepressible

irresponsibility,
the two Freest people in Colorado,
at least on August 9th, 2016, I overhear the mellifluous
tongue of a mother with her
two-year-old daughter & twelve-year-old son
waft between both
Spanish & American
saying to her own mother that
she ordered a margarita at a bar & it was pure
alcohol burning her throat so she couldn't take it,

& I laughed outloud
asking where that was 'cause
that's my kind of drink all of us laughing at the difference
in taste — The Hacienda in Colorado Springs,
which fact we filed for future reference,
& although I'd waved sweet nothings
at little Iris,
didn't want young Tomas to go
ignored & complimented

him on his cap
with a capital "P"
+ diagonal line through
it he said wasn't a Phillies
cap like his uncle thought, but
"Primitive,"
which got me to talking
about the importance of the Prime
& Primitive in my work: caves
& petroglyphs & Native Americans

to which he proudly swung
his right hand all around pointing

to each of them at the table, Mother, Diana,
little Sis, Iris,
& to himself, of course, finally
aiming toward his Grandmother, Maria Lourdes,
who immediately claimed
her Cherokee heritage
on the American
side & Aztec on the Mexican,

which we took in slowly
listening to every shared word
what with it soothing the remnants of the wound
of the cell & bad Muzak competing for cacophony,
that when finished,
I had to share the coincidence
of what I was just writing, Kerouac
wearing the clothes of a man found on a dump,
not knowing whether the guy
was dead or alive,
but I didn't allude to the desire
of his girlfriend in the letter
Jack also found in the bag,
what with her looking for enough money
to buy a tablecloth, asking for 10 cents, contrasting
that to any American woman having to ask
"money for such a humble,
useful purpose," rather
I told them,
Diana, Tomas,
little Iris, & Maria Lourdes,
I had to head home to finish what I'd started
before we all talked,
& would make sure I mentioned
each of them in the piece,
smiles all around
as they say in the same language.

HEAR FROM NONE

Hear from none
      for three days
           one grows
used to
     it, refuses
         to succumb,
recruits the mountains,
      if not only their cold form
           as company much resembling
such absence.

Tie laces of oldest boots.
      Kale soup finished boiling.
         Randomly off the radio
comes Miles Davis's
    - *Nuit sur les Champs-Élysées (take 3)*
              (a.k.a. Générique),
which & whom
     I recognize,
        listen to,
& believe in.

HOW CAN A MAN TROUBLE HIMSELF TOWARD LONELINESS?

Saw sunrise as slowly as I rose this morning
on the 22nd day
of my 70th birthday,
which event didn't go
unrecognized by wife, daughters,
friends, foothills, Pikes in the distance,
& the great need to jot letters down here, there.

Everywhere: seven bottles of wine daughter sent
& said, were each for the decade I'd made it through.

So downed white Burgundy throughout the night.
How can a man trouble himself toward
loneliness, when he has such entities
orbiting round him? One sin he
blatantly commits & ought
to quit, & abandon.

However, I'll narrow
that loneliness down
further to a sense of mere
isolation harking back
etymologically
to the Latin *insulatus*,
to be made into an island,
which this territory has done,
one man an island
in between
mountains.

STANDING SILENT AT ED DORN'S GRAVE

Music of the literal & candor.
Fled down newly named Buffalo Highway
in pilgrimage to Dorn's grave
at Green Mountain Cemetery first
talking with Mary Miller, who left
Manzanola at 2:30 in the morning
with her grandson, Seth, traveling through
Pueblo, Wigwam, & Fountain, up past
Colorado Springs in order to freight
lamb parts from the Triple M Bar Ranch
to the Boulder farmers market by 6:30
yesterday & every Saturday, while husband
David traveled even further than those
180 miles all the way up to Longmont.

Dorn went Paleo long before it went
fashionable eating meat only keeping
his gun toting hips slim.
Mary & Seth kept both hearts, both tongues,
both livers cold for me, while we browsed
the other tents for green beans, one yellow tomato,
loaf of seven-grain, & round of goat cheese.
Picked up the organs, put them in the cooler
in the trunk of the car, & walked
to Red Letter Books to see if I could
score a couple more books like last time
with *Recollections of Gran Apacheria*,
which another Seth brought out from behind
the desk when he saw me take down Clark's bio.

But, no, Seth wasn't around, although this other
dude claimed to be good friends
with Ed's son Kidd,
but didn't know
the whereabouts of the grave.

Then, when I mentioned meeting Dorn
in Richard Grossinger's kitchen
up at Goddard,
dude says he's best friends
with *his son*, Abe,
& visited them in their gated community
in Hollywood.

I stopped trying to get a word in
edgewise, while Kathleen talked to the bookstore
patron, Stephanie, who volunteered
to give directions
to the cemetery,
saying her husband wanted
to be buried there.

(Kathleen just came back
from her Sunday morning walk smelling of earth,
so fresh, this Colorado earth
scent on her very flesh!!)

So at odds with the grave
we got to situated as it is right
under the Flatirons as Guardians of the Dead.

She found it,
appropriately enough in the section,
Garden of Knowledge, walking behind all the stones
keeping an eye out for the poem
engraved on the back reading,
This tapestry moves / as the morning lights up.

There was the first silence all around
to be found in the entire state of Colorado
on the second last day of July since moving into our new digs
on the last day of June,
a long time to be without a single drop

…

of silence
as the silence flowed
below the Flatirons, streamed
second-by-second until seconds
melted into something beyond time
seeping underground
as Dorn's poem outspoke any
silent prayer either of us intended
to offer up, or down,
turning into a clarity of mourning.

Standing above various pure white quartz
laid down by others
on the granite gravestone
in homage, along with the lone
shot glass holding half a shot
of recent rain.

AS MEN IN DENVER

She's over there on Cody,
I'm here on Custer.
She hasn't driven
once since we've been here
42 days all tolled.

It's good to see Dorn
here younger than I am
now
evincing a similar attitude
about the place & the people,
similar to hers, too, as she spits
out the word hate at the most
inopportune time while I'm driving.

Dorn says bicyclists
& motorists
of Boulder
would just as soon pin your
mother to the asphalt, or
brother
sister
cat
dog,
but squirrels they'll chase up a tree!!

My experience on the highways
here in Denver, points West,
& all points in between
dictate: *She ain't drivin'!!*
Ed's take on I-80
is so revelatory,
where truckers
of every which rig
are cowboys without

...

a cow in sight,
merciless,
but there's something
about this wild
West we both
like as men
in Denver.

The challenge
he says the place is
tougher than Beirut,
which is no
hyperbole.
Dorn kept to his guns,
as they say, in life & work.
No words holstered. Joy at his
sense of humor, while my shillelagh
remains on the floor in the backseat, hands
on wheel, only our tongues still making a fist.

BELIEVING THEY'RE THE REAL THING

It reads & one is
pleased not
to compare the page to other
known lines,
but accept the minor category,
the ring, rhythm
as an undermining masterpiece
against that which any other that
would claim monumentality.

On our way home from the Garden
of the Gods there in Colorado Springs,
where granted, old town matched
Bear Skin Neck
in Rockport where I first lived,
for Kitch.

The trip back
from the Garden
(have I mentioned that many
more days & nights than once
twice hundreds of times
I've found myself
with less than five dollars?)

the road home offered
the opportunity of a lifetime
for someone from a long line
of provincial Easterners:
three young men
on horseback herding
well over two hundred head
of black cattle
there in what they call

...

Greenland, Colorado,

our first sight
of real cowboys
doing real work other
than these dudes with dark
beards in pick-up trucks (Dorn
has a name for
them in ***Abhorrences***)

speeding
down the same
highway thinking,
not thinking believing
they're the real thing.

AS THE NEON MOON NEARS

There's a bit of mourning
the loss of the poet or
writer one returns
to revisiting pages,
as I'm doing
yet again tonight,
as the neon
moon nears
full & crosses at midnight
just above this other
scholar's reading
lamp.

DOUBTS ABOUT HOW OFTEN ONE WORD CAN STAND ALONE

Doubts about how often one word
can stand alone as a line in a work of art
poetry's supposed to rise up, or down to, but
will catch attempts at times reading the genre.

Drove straight through all the traffic lights dotting
Alameda into Denver 210 South Broadway to be exact:
Fahrenheits Books where Bill had first editions of Miller's
Cosmological Eye & a Viking '57 **On the Road** behind glass,

but couldn't track down the slender volume I wanted
by Ed Dorn published by Harvey Brown in West Newbury,
Mass of all places in 1971 around the time I met him, his Frontier
Press way ahead of the game getting not only Dorn's work out, Jones,

Olson, Pound, & from what I gather, not only that, produced
music by Don Cherry, Clifford Brown, & Ornette Coleman.
South Broadway has fragments of the Old Soul of Denver.
Next door in the Book Mall found a pulp Ballantine copy

of Kerouac's **Lonesome Traveler** with cover photo
by Robert Frank along with the Avon **Maggie Cassidy**
with the topless blonde on the cover in the arms
of muscular Jack.

LENGTHY LONGEVITY OF THE DREAM

Rollicking good party
in the dream, a long way
from any such event in real life,
perhaps a memory,
or wish.
At any rate, crowded,
& now
that I think of it probably influenced
by the group
of young people gathered
together in the lobby of the Hotel Colorado,
including jazz band with fine drummer,
pianist, sax, even euphonium
which I'd never seen
nor heard of
before.

At some point
a young man came in
with what appeared to be coal dust
on his face,
except for where
he may have worn a mask
previously there in the depth
of the dream mine.

Damn, really, there
was that hundred-car coal train heading West
on our return trip home
to Denver's Union Station.

I must have tried to imagine
what'd be like there in that dark,

recalling the depth
of the hold
in the Japanese factory ship
in Gloucester, & how hard it was
to stack 77.5 lb.
boxes of frozen
fish ten high
on pallets hoisted up & out by crane,
fast forklifted into the warehouse
for storage, eventually
trucked down to the Fort's old Birdseye plant,
or up the hill to Gorton's.

Who the Hell would guess the dream would take me all the way
there?

Dock foreman,
Mr. Patrican, said,
during the brief half-hour lunch
(during which I had no lunch),
but sweated profusely head down
sitting on the dock,
"We had a guy here from Pennsylvania,
who worked in the coalmines there claimed this
job harder than that one."

It wasn't the young man
with coal dust on his face
looked me over
wondering what could account
for the discrepancy
in age between me & all the young folk
dominating the partygoers,
so just as I'd told the kids in the jazz band
that I'd seen Miles in '69
still angry over King's murder,
told this guy in the dream seemingly mystified by age,
that Tomas Tranströmer,

whom I once met at his apartment
in Boston told me it paid to hang out
with youth, that
that physicality, cells' & genes' energy
(just wrote *evergy*)
turned Spirit
entered the Soul
of everyone within
proximity converting
any conversation there, the exchange
in words, or even silence shared turned
seconds, minutes, Time itself
into a potential, lengthy
longevity.

AT THIS ELEVATION

Adore seeing, hearing, breathing, tasting, caressing
the wind the trees, leaves, birds, & I enjoy & marvel
at this elevation where purity & clarity of air is something
I'm not used to nor experienced to any great length, except
perhaps train ride with Matterhorn mere thorn in Swiss Alps sky.

Or say, Oaxaca, Guadalajara, even Mexico City over
forty-two years ago, or on the same trip down before that,
Flagstaff, Arizona, where two pair of Wild Turkey crossing
the highway remain the most colorful of animals ever encountered.
Strong, gusty wind today in Colorado blessing trees, leaves, birds, & me.

STRAIGHT TO BOONE

Already addressed the lodgepole pine
as it climbed up past a second story
window of the motel we squatted
at during a previous visit out
West, marveling then at its
limbless stature & former
use in construction of
Native American
tipis, what the
British also
call ridge-
pole pine
while

the Oxford Dictionary cites Teddy Roosevelt as first
person to utter
the name.

Now a German forest ranger claims trees
are social beings able *to warn each other of potential danger,
nurse sick neighbors, count, learn, & remember...*

Across the way here, part of the Foothills, a quaking aspen's
been signaling me something since dawn,
calls up hearing a recording of Dorn
reading that poem of his in Vancouver, 1963,
Death While Journeying, where he places
Meriwether Lewis at Natchez Trace,*"
(strangely alluding to the period as one hundred years before
psychoanalysis, of all things)
riding horseback to see his dying mother.
Dorn admits that

*Taken direct & obliquely from Katherine Coman's 1912 *Economic Beginnings of the Far West* suggested by Olson.

...

the piece is a use of historical
material that simply excited him.
I know that charge.
Thing is, that when Ed got toward
the end of the reading, after
the brilliant image of Lewis with his back to the continent,
& the key word in the poem, demise,
arrives he glosses over it
straight to Boone.

SUCH LINGUISTIC IMPRINTS

One gets so practiced, that even
when climbing a mountain, each step of ascent
from walk to hike to climb are such linguistic
imprints no pen or paper
need record purple
glistening of initial foothill
sedge, or massive little grasshopper
sunbathing in the calyx
of a black-eyed Susan,
nor at the halfway point, where cactus
shows itself parallel
to the first ancient cistern
hard-carved out of volcanic tufa
left behind by the glacier.

By the time treeline presents cone-filled pines
to combine air of elevation
begin to cool one down
as boots trudge over
scree & roots,
it's true,
we entered the back end of the mountain
from the cemetery leaving Dorn & Berlin there
under stone markers & lines
from their work: *Tapestry & Time; heartache & bones*
in their own way
still urging us on up past
a 2nd larger cistern all eight wells
holding not water,
but stray stones,
old pine needles,
& the aura of language
left behind.

NOW, HERE, AUGUST 16TH IN COLORADO

Back in Maine our little Cape
had Bay windows that looked out
at a massive Victorian used to be a funeral parlor.
Once in a while a full moon would climb its way past the alley
created by wrap-around front porch, clapboards, overhanging roof
& huge stand of towering oaks:
rare occasion.

Now, here, August 16th in Colorado
with two picture windows
on top of each other in the living room,
yet another in the loft, I can't help
getting up in the middle of the night
& wandering around the floor like some celestial
wayfarer.

Two nights ago
something drew me
toward the closest window,
after observing digital clocks
all around reading 2:03, whereupon
due West the moon balanced on one peak
of the Front Range, as if it just might topple over.

No, I stood there watching it keep its balance,
then slowly roll down the other side,
not hurting a single tree,
until a full four minutes later it reached
its destination out of sight. In its wake, Saturn
came into view, Antares broke out of the darkness,
& in succession, South to West: Mars, Spica, Jupiter, Mercury,
& lower & last, but not least, Venus.

WAXING TO WANING

Worked through the night,
not on the clock for any remuneration
per usual, catching a glimpse of full moon
during a brief break from this thankless task.

But I enjoyed putting pieces together,
the urge from within for right character,
syllable, phrase, intense thrust of each discrete
sentence.

During which time, unbeknownst to me,
moon went from waxing to waning.
Caught a similar visage in the mirror
just before bed, not caring about age,

earned mine on the page.

EVEN SCRATCHES HEARD ON VINYL ARE OF USE

If it won't, for us, turn into a rhythm
for language, then useless
to us, but so few
are there here
useless, this ice
I place in ceramic cup
add wine to is of such use
on an August afternoon under
sweltering 97-degree skies I bless
this ice melting right before my eyes.

This steamer trunk standing vertically
in the corner of the new living room
balancing the radio, where *Budo*
just blared against fine acoustic
walls I recognized as Miles's
tune off *Birth of the Cool*
from 1957, when I was
eleven, & just heard
scratches on vinyl, bless
them too, on the following tune:
Sonny Rollins, "Body & Soul" from *Big Brass*.

Balls, I'd add to that last title, & stack of empty
banana & apple boxes in the bedroom toted
my entire library over 2,000 miles 'cross
country she refuses to store or throw
away hoping return East will
occur sooner than later, if
she sinks far enough
into a nostalgic
Blue for New
England.

Dig the vertical rhythm, percussive nature of steamer
trunks under jazz radio & empty banana & apple
boxes she hopes will once again tote valuable
books back to what she believes is home,
& I tune into her Blue mood & try my
best to console her Soul, Bless her
Soul, who is the most animate
& rhythmic, practical thing
imaginable beyond
trunks, boxes, ice,
wine in ceramic
cup.

LESSENING THE EVERYDAY HEAVINESS

Times it's a good life,
a poet's, struggles lessen, lift,
as if elevation lightened the air
& heaviness of the expressive load.

Silence accompanies one, no solo, so
simply look, after peering inside, outside
where mountains whisper in the wind carrying
the primitive message of wild calm.

One's own culture surrounds one on myriad
bookshelves, or intervening, sudden memory
of single frame in admired film, Bertolucci *Stealing Beauty*
from willing & naïve Liv Tyler.

Then, a friend shares a photo of the moon
slowly setting over Fitz Hugh Lane's
home in Gloucester, & randomly, immediately
spontaneous, since mountain air in Denver is light,

& gravity abates for another brief moment, yes,
struggles lessen temporarily, when one opens to a page
in a new copy of an old book marked *Par Avion*
from a friend abroad knows these lines by heart

allowing Charles to speak for both of us & all
in a rare horizontal example
(horizon actually visible)
of his verse:

Lane's eye-view of Gloucester
Phoenician eye-view…

& I breathe sighs of relief, via his voice & Lane's palette,

at the lightening of such gravity, lessening
the everyday heaviness
of this poet's expressive enterprise.

QUIET SHOUTOUT FOR A LONGTIME FRIEND

At the turn
of the digital
clock just past
nine a.m. Red Garland
dominates the atmosphere
on piano in here within Coltrane's
1958 *Stardust*, while secretly, newly
out of the shower, she dons blue
underpants & black bra.

Coffee's on.
Mountains still talking
to me through open windows
on a Denver day hopes to reach record
temp of 78 this November day when friend,
Peter Anastas, who also played Jazz
piano; only Classical Greek Scholar
at Bowdoin College back in the day;
when that still meant something;
Florence in his future;
celebrates another
birthday.

Look at these shadows between
Venetian-blind light scrape
diagonally down high
22-foot walls.
Look, I say.
He & I are still alive!!
Listen, it's Booker Ervin
on tenor sax from the album
The Freedom Book.

Our lives a prayer along lines
toward duration.

PULLING INTO GRANBY

As you pull into Granby, Colorado don't
get your hopes up at the sign for Pioneer Motel,
which sign is elevated,
granted, on two towering
steel poles one can observe
from the road a good distance away,
but when you get there
underneath the letters
each one historically intact,
there's nothing
but scrub without
even any evidence
of the foundation long
abandoned.

However, further on
down the same trail
Rocky Mountain Collision
seems to be doing a stellar business
with its massive pile of rubber tires
covering most of the glacial scree
in the ravine
behind the garage,
while prior to Granby itself wide acres of pasture
populated with many
a prancing young Angus heifer appear
to exhibit much more carefree
enthusiasm up here at 7,935 feet
for life than this town has
seen in decades.

TO MAKE IT HOME

In the dream last night I had to drive
three people to the park to walk,

then realized I'd left license & wallet
back home, so instead of joining them

for the nighttime exercise, no less,
dropped them off, turned the car around.

But the dream environment was unfamiliar.
Slowed down at the end of the road to read

the street sign: <u>Self Street</u>. I'd have to make
it home, then back here to take a right on

<u>Self Street</u> in order to pick up the others
on time. Huge cement truck or noisy

street sweeper driven by a woman yielded
the right of way, when all of a sudden

I skated on the balls of my feet, or small
wheels under my boots hurrying past crowds

of people, mostly men, leaving church or
group meetings. I sped. Dodged.

Steady as she goes down this long wide thoroughfare
of Route 97. Now, just yesterday I'd looked up

the old Salem Depot I used to tag along to pick
up my Aunt Irene coming home from work

as a legal secretary in Lynn, Massachusetts.
Built in 1847, a few years later Hawthorne alluded

to its *spacious breadth, & an airy height from floor to roof…*

I knew if I could locate the dream train station
I could find my way home, & there it was, the current

one, on the left, whereupon I turned & asked a woman,
"What's the name of this street?"

"Norway Avenue," she answered. I could wend my way back
to <u>Self Street</u> by banging that last right at the end of Norway,

resonating so similarly in sound in my waking ears
to <u>No Way</u>.

ANTARES STARES DOWN

Pushed time past the four a.m. hour
    traipsed barefoot across the floor
to close the window
below freezing,
    when that star
glistened in
the Southern Sky
    reminding me there
        & then that here I am
            closer to the celestial realm
than ever before.

OUR NEWEST PATH

We've got our newest path: where once it scraped the outer reaches
of Cape Ann, natural granite rock pool
in front of the Cook's place on
Eastern Point
warm enough in March to dive into & swim across,
or the cave out there we hid
in huddled, coupled;
say Oceanside Drive, Scituate all
the way to the lighthouse & back perhaps along the parallel seawall;
or Portland from the International Ferry Terminal
to East End Beach,
cliff stones, scree strewn below,
in archaeological discourse
with jagged shoreline detritus keeping ocean at bay.

No, now it's this little ragged disconnect of shallow lakes they call 'em,
not quite stagnant, where we hunt
for anything at all resembling the natural world
like yesterday when we caught
the Great Blue Heron out of corner
of our eyes landing on man-made perch in the middle of the largest
body of water,
or after proving to her
a Kingfisher survived there, she walked over solo
& saw the bird speed low-level
from one end
of said lagoon to another,
interpreting it all by her lonesome
as good omen.

SO CIVIL, THE SEVEN OF THEM

Got up early from the trouble
on mind would have continued
to wrestle with, if I hadn't taken note
of the horizon prior to sunrise,
where Ravens matched
that line East to West, larger than crows
back home, recalling the flock
of them yesterday on our walk so civil,
the seven of them over
the corpse
of the little chipmunk, astonishing
really, to witness such
lack of rancor,
not an angry wingbeat, nor
audible squawk, so that when I took
out the lamb liver from the freezer I thought
of that colloquy of birds,
how little we leave them
& that minor carrion
compared to what now appeared
so large this organ
with perfect liminal contours
& scent rising up as I ran it under
cold water I can't take either at all
for granted.

ITALIAN ARCHITECT FROM ANOTHER CENTURY

Italian architect from another century
entered the dream
with a cane
hobbling on a deformed right ankle,
handsome for his age,
which I inquired about just as he turned
the corner stage left.

"Sixty-two," replied
the centuries-old man.

Astonished, I kept my astonishment
to my dream self, but he pivoted
back around on that bad ankle
in order to double-check
my checked reaction.

Simply uttered, "Oh," I reassured him.

Trailed him toward his upstairs office, "Professor,
would you like a cup fish stew, I have some
leftover at home?"

Which was true from the actual
day before, but when I returned
home only fish remained, broth
evaporated.

Knew I had wine in the fridge, & a bottle
of Bar Harbor clam broth in the cupboard,
when suddenly a long line of old friends appeared,
telling them all I could doctor the soup
for the famous Italian architect,

at the same time noticed him standing
among those old friends overhearing my plans
to remedy the original offer,
my own postmodern
dream blueprint.

DRIVING INTO THE DAY ALL THE WAY FROM THE NIGHT BEFORE

We were both more or less not well from the night
before, so I took over the wheel in the snow
the whole way past Colfax to Cody
knowing the only cure when we
got to the destination was pure
water & renowned kale soup.
She smiled, we hugged,
snow continued down
dry as only fourteen

degree temperatures &
mountain elevation can
make it. Off-white as driven-in
snow. What we craved was a beer.
Or glass of red wine, anything other than
that five-year-old Broadbent Madeira from
the night before. Of course, around here <u>things
can always get worse</u>: ominous fire engine outside
the office of the Golden Hours Motel on West Colfax.

MY IMMEDIATE VISION

Five, don't bother
counting, they come
visually & separately in
intuitive in number,
midges clinging
for their dear
lives to
window screens
escaping random
November snowflakes,
when days before,
invisible there
was nothing
in between
to distract
my immediate vision
from clouds & sun
illuminating
Foothills
in the distance.

LEAPING CLIFF LEDGE TO GLACIAL ERRATICS

> *I am the Gold Machine and now I have trenched out,*
> *smeared occupied....* — Charles Olson

Yesterday's applauding of the distinction
between species of Ravens & crows,
although smaller, the latter is no
less intelligent, & as I read how
the largest common Raven
will seek out a ledge or
crack in cliff face,
the male will deliver building
materiel, while the female constructs
the nest. The female Chihuahuan Raven
creates a deep cup in the ground with her breast
by a series of push/prod near ancient dance moves.

This new information had me harking back
to my days in Gloucester, where after working
nights for a year at the Birdseye frozen fish plant
on the Fort
overlooking Pavilion Beach
(not a single window to look out of) cutting slabs
of frozen fish
fresh off factory
ships out of Russia & Japan,
we banked that check for our trek
to Mexico, where I gave myself four
months to pass my own writing test.

Passed it down there in Veracruz on the typewriter
Manuel Avila Camacho provided, & returned
home to sell our cottage overlooking
Fernwood Lake in West Gloucester
living on the proceeds.

...

Just so happens
we moved into servants quarters
above the carriage house on the Birdseye Estate,
where on one side sun set
over the harbor, on the other rose
over Brace Cove.

You could find me on the docks
in town with notebook
& a bottle of wine in my Army shoulder bag.

But wouldn't see me leaping cliff ledge to glacial erratics
all along the furthest reaches of that spit of land
Smith named Tragabigzanda
after his mistress in Istanbul.

No, the only other man
I'd encounter on Brace Cove,
while Bemo Ledge roared against the waves,
was the guy who fed crows,
& who told me once one
dropped a shiny dime
at his feet in gratitude.

CALLIGRAPHIC SIGN *GUANG*

On our way West for appointments
with Dean of Business School,
& others, I'll carry the image
down Buffalo Highway
in my head the calligraphic sign
Guang, to visit, to ramble, picturing
as it does: King in Boat with Dog
at Stern so any vehicle exhaust
is rather wake
of water.

We'll keep those meetings
on time, along with haphazard
greetings with what seemed like the entire
library staff: Skip in reference to David in Archives,
Deborah in Special Collections all the way up
to Dean Williams in his office,
who knows Gloucester
& Dogtown,
shakes my hand
firmly three times
before my heading out
the door to the English Department

& Jeffrey DeShell to drop off
Animated Landscape,
Olson/Still: Crossroad,
& Janus Head with poems
solicited from Sidney Goldfarb,
who used to teach there, good friend
of Ed Dorn's,
whose grave will be our final stop before sailing home.

...

ii.

Ya, we'll say our goodbyes
to young Jack & River
at Hotel Boulderado,
then Mary, Lamb
Lady, & Rod
at the farmers' market
between Canyon & Arapahoe,
the latter ready to deliver another five tons of food to those
protesting at Standing Rock
against oil pipeline
private interests
plan to shove under
the Missouri in North Dakota.

It's all about
(don't mix) oil, + water
CEO of Nestlé, Peter Brabeck, says
is not a human right.

Water, CEO of Nestlé, Peter
Brabeck, says is not a human right.

Water, CEO of Nestlé,
Peter Brabeck, says is not a human right.

Chant it!
As if dancing round a blazing campfire: Water,
CEO of Nestlé, Peter Brabeck, says is not a human right.

Water, CEO of Nestlé, Peter Brabeck, says is not a human right.

The rhythm's right right now,
so I'll tell you what I saw on our last day there

in Boulder, Colorado
at One Boulder Plaza,1801 13th Street primitively hallucinogenic
right before these postmodern eyes: looked down,
there & now,
to what's pulled up
out of slate: = cow in first stage
of birth giving birth to calf, water
membrane spilled intact just below her
on the ground.

Track it down.

WHAT THE SUN IS DOING

for **Jim Feast & Nancy Chung**

Weekend disappeared behind sundown,
Foothills, & waxing crescent moon practically
carrying Venus on deck like a Gloucester schooner.

This Monday morning has her out & about soothing
our daughter's wounded Soul. I've got the southern sun
to my back, our solar-six-picture windows keeping the place

warm without turning on the heat. Nearest window surrounded
by a string of hot red chili pepper holiday lights half-off
Saturday at Goodwill, while staircase leading to loft

is strung with green blue red yellow & an array of gold
balls, four brandishing cowboy boots as Christmas
stockings. Coleman Hawkins comes on with

Quintessence, as if he knew her, too, enough
to Love & Praise. Look at what the sun is doing
now over & above the steamer trunk in the corner:

Cosmos barging in.

HER RHYTHMIC TONE

Magpie on Cody Street mailbox
foreshadowed word from a number
of friends. Now Coleman Hawkins on
tenor riffing "Just Friends", while I'm hid away
here out West knowing no one. But swallows see me,
& the Woman the mountain makes keeps quiet company
coaxing sunrise up & sunset down.

I listen in.
Pick up only
her rhythmic tone.

WESTERN FRONTIER EXPERIMENT

We're aware that
after today, shortest
of the year, sunrise
we've been witnessing
for so many mornings
will appear to turn back
around South to North,
& begin to number our
days remaining, as if it
hasn't always already,
but days hours minutes
seconds & fragments
of them, begin to chase
us back East, toss us up
& out of these mountains,
sun marking the inevitable
trek march migration,
however much begrudge
it, away from this ephemeral
Western frontier experiment.

ECLIPSE, DENVER, DECEMBER 13, 2016

Here in Denver I look out at the strength
& power of the Stars piercing
full Moon's light,
which will set
at 6:30 a.m.
Sunrise at 7:13.
But a shudder at the frailty
of Earth passes by like an eclipse.

TONIGHT: THE SMALL BUT DISTINCTIVE
CONSTELLATION, CORVUS

The abyss is
not bottomless,
but there are corpuscles
flowing through capillaries
& history yet to come visible
in turmoil to the extent it's river,
or stream, current, & one had best,
rather than leap into, nor step back
from it, hover above it by those entities
dream said are sent down from crow's landing.

Friday, December 23, 2016

RAVEN

Raven, I see him where he was & where he's going,
craves the last light flying high above the mountains
at the end of each day to catch the other side of sundown.

GIVING BIRTH TO ANOTHER DAY

Walk up the staircase to the loft
for no other
reason than exercise
on the morning before the holiday at the end of
December, & look
at the horizon
over Denver
that Sun rose over just after
7:20 this morning
creeping now back
North as it has been three days running
since Solstice,
the Woman in the Mountain giving birth
to another Winter's Day.
Kathleen out for a power walk,
while I have to clean off
the Yale Library Table
of 19 books
& newly purchased handwritten
letter by Edward Dorn from Colchester, UK, there
in 1966, that
interim year between
witnessing Nobel Prize Laureate
Dylan go electric
& three months hitchhiking 'round Europe with stops
in London Dover Calais Arras
Brussels Amsterdam Rotterdam
Bremen København Helsingør
Berlin Munich Salzburg Rijeka
Split Dubrovnik Venice Rome
Capri (are you still with me?)

Livorno Genoa Nice Cannes
Coursegoules Montjoux Paris

Amiens Calais Dover London
New York Boston Home, which
when I complete the journey via
this text list, Kathleen walks in
as if to validate her presence
as Home itself anywhere on this earth,
The Woman in the Mountain
& the Sun giving birth
to another day.

MONDAY

What is poetry, other
than constant reminder
of constant tactile fingertips:
letters, each letter, vowel & consonant,
or HOWL, ALLEN, DAMN,
I'm more or less upside down
on the leather loveseat
out of Amsterdam
living room picture window
& loft hovering
might have a cough but not
uncool if
she comes by with a kiss
in upside down
just like the Chagall
on *Birthday*, 1915, above
my Monday Mystic
head…

AT THE TURN, PEERING INTO DORN'S WORLD

3:59 in the morning
killing Time first
Time in life,
waiting on
Winter Solstice
24 hours minus
15 minutes away,
surfing the Net
for info on Dorn,
already gone through
texts during daylight,
this darkness adds
mystery to Ed's descent
genetics bones skin
tongue voice breath
color genealogy meeting
his old man one Time
exchanging letters
regarding love & money
exposing the tear
in the natural
fabric of estranged
chromosomes.

FINDING VENUS EMBEDDED DEEP IN INDIGO

Up & at it right away
from dreams had me
back East on the coast,
even on a boat, second
one had me with captain,
or mate, negotiating price
& freshness of fish, while
first one on land must have
been market, shellfish only
aplenty.

Now before 5:30 a.m. wide
awake, barefoot at that,
on cold linoleum just
to make the coffee, kitchen
lit only by gooseneck
reading lamp totally
out of place.

Sucked coffee scent in but good,
knowing she'd be pleased finishing
task in eight-day-old winter
cold out West.
On the way back
to bed detouring in order to check sky for stars
find Venus embedded deep in Indigo
reminding me so much of ink
practiced as kids on lonely
desks we'd write on & keep
bagged lunch in before
advent of crowded
cafeteria halls.

Now, a short eleven hours later
Time's bright daylight combines
with low-lying valley chill
to *shroud* nearby Foothills
weather forecasters refuse
to call fog simply
(limited visibility)
what with each ridge
at any distance seen
clear through
to it all.

UNKNOWN

Woman in the Mountain wide
awake on the second day of the New Year,
while I slept & dreamt
of Cambridge, about to buy
a topcoat for 600 bucks,
but closed on Mondays, reverted
to an apartment there,
maybe visited early on
back then with Robert Hellman,
that kind of literary & welcoming milieu,
the four of us on the floor scanning a poem titled,
"Joys of Communication" in which key
word, *unknown,* had us wondering whether
it should be
qualified
or left to stand alone?

My newfound friends
thought it should be
elaborated upon.
I felt mystery
should be allowed
to remain.
Wanted to make a phone call,
but couldn't recall
the Area Code for Rockport,
where Hellman & I hung out before
he flew off for København,
teaching part-time at the university
squatting in Nørrebro.
Squatting, homeless,
that huge fear of mine,
compensated upon

Big Time
in the dream with new friends in Cambridge,
where in real life I recently applied
for a job at my age
I guess out of fear
of squatting,
homeless,
unknown.

TIME, AS SEPARATE

Begun to love,
      guess that's it,
Time   as separate
      entity, both near & distant
here in the mountains, whereas for years

Time
      inhabited my body
(we, she & I, continue to wake or sleep & dream
      that way), but once
awake to day & night

Time   becomes discrete.
Today I prepared kale soup in defense
      against four degree
below
      Zero temps.

It wasn't much.
          Something I'm used to,
comforting.   To do it right,
(won't bother with entire recipe here),
      takes a good hour

& a half of preparation, cutting
      veins out of kale leaves,
double-washing,
      tossing in whatever
else is on hand,

in this case broccoli, leftover
sweet bell peppers,
      quarter head of cauliflower, withered

bunch of collard greens, etc.,
now that I think of it: couple Yukon gold potatoes.

   It's still simmering...
              Walked over to leather couch by the window
rest weary legs & simply stare
                    at blanket of overnight snow,
digging shadows' branches

                  of locust tree across the way
remade itself across length of carport roof,
                        practically
the only nonwhite lines making vivid capillary
                 impressions on my mind.

Suddenly, a lone white bird flies overhead in between
                    white ground & white sky.
Unidentified, reaches
                             massive cupola
on neighborhood apartment complex,

                            naturally

    symbolic, I thought
Time
    not internal, no longer corpuscular,
                              but still

of inestimable invaluable
       in the instant,
             to be grasped, apart,
                      savored,
                            & let go.

CRISSCROSSINGS

Hear tell snow's
about to fall back East
as we prepare our return
playing tennis
all afternoon under
crisscrossings
high above
left by jets,
connected as we are
at an altitude
we'll surely miss.

On the way home zoom
in on both Plains Cottonwoods
at the corner of South Kipling
& West Alameda
entwined
in a way
scientists
would call a loving,
protective
embrace.

Ten months in one place isn't long
enough for human beings
to put down roots,
so we'll take as many
lasting images as possible,
deposit them in memory
so back East over snow,
strolling banks of the Kennebec,
this sky, those limbs
can crop up
beside us.

SUN & SMOKE

Sun taking its own good time curving
over Foothills heading
toward Spring
Equinox at 4:28 a.m.
Mountain on the 20th
ten days from now on
a Monday, while today,
Friday, fire continues to burn
more than 66 acres of South Table
Mountain getting dangerously close
to the scar dug for the 2010 Silver Bullet
blaze, which if it gets any nearer residents
will have to evacuate.

Rather, the main concern
out here, where you can smell
the smoke, is proximity to the Coors
plant at the heart of Golden's
economy,
but of course,
in this day & age,
it's not like the massive
corporate edifice is some Last
Chance Saloon made of soft Plains
Cottonwood timber, iron nails,
& pitch,
is it?

SIGN & SYMBOL

We were there
comparing current
digs to those long past.

She preferred those houses.
I favored apartments, when
of a sudden the fish cloud rose

up out the window, then moments
later antelope, whereupon I suggested
such signs for primitive man & woman

here in the West meant something more
before knowing it was mere water & mist.
Seriously, I did prefer sign for fish & antelope

way above symbol for covalent
bonding of two parts hydrogen,
one part oxygen.

THAT WAS THEN

When we head
to the five bodies
of water for our walk
first thing you see is Golden,
Colorado in the distance with its
multi-million dollar homes encroaching
up the mountainside.

During our initial
hunt for a place to live
outside the confines of our
daughter's & son-in-law's basement
apartment, we made the mistake of driving
up there. One of the neighbors, just one, mind
you, dared stand outside talking to a cop in his cruiser.

I dared park
the car, & approached.
Excused myself, letting both
know we were new to Colorado
all the way from Maine the past week,
looking for someplace to live. Cop kept
his head down at computer hoping for word

of any criminal activity
hadn't happened near there
in years, while homeowner bragged
there was nothing around, NOTHING,
& that property values here had soared more
than in any other part of the country, his smirk
a fine gesture of Western hospitality.

That was then.

OUR MEMORY ALONE

She saw it as mist draped down, that gauze,
between us & mountains in the near distance,
I saw fog. Regardless, it's moved on or burned
off by now. All so new & unfamiliar we're bound
to be mistaken about one thing or another.

For example, that Red-tailed hawk yesterday
hovering obliquely, not exactly above all
that relentless careless traffic hustling down
Wadsworth Boulevard, the one we wanted
to take as sign, good omen.

Couldn't really justify it as such, what with
what seemed no open land underneath her,
simply sprawl, all those corporate franchises
I damnwell refuse to name. Now that hawk
hovers above nothing, but our memory alone.

BLUE HANDS, GREY JACKET

Blue hands, grey jacket
on inside the cold house.

Forty-eight degrees
out. Pour more

black coffee.
Bye Bye Blackbird

with Miles & Coltrane
came on during the initial

commute this morning at the exact second
the shaggy white dog

of Death stared straight into me
demanding change, or else, just

as Rilke's own white marble had.
So sure, I'll cut my hair

today for the first time in months,
& maybe even skip the wine tonight.

By the main drag caught sight of three blackbirds
in the sky hassling a lone crow.

As if the whole scenario were
some phenomenal confirmation.

THE WIND SANG

Wind overnight kept these close-
to deaf ears
company to the extent that I had to climb
(what a beautiful word that
is suddenly
to look at,
say, even
with its
own silent "b") climb loft stairs to be
nearer high winds, where night
was as black to me
as it's ever been,
& the wind
sang rather than spoke,
lulled rather than rocked,
so that now I'm thrown back
(she's still whistling her daytime tune)
to the chair looked out the kitchen window of grandparents'
2nd floor apartment on Winthrop Street in Salem, where
the adults left me alone,
for once, & I looked
adoringly at the tree
in the neighbors' yard
appreciating its singularity,
& my own.

ELEVEN LINES OF ADORATION

With Pikes shrouded
by clouds into disappearance,
wind doing more
than its usual
whispers, I detect
a sense of joy in sound,
& stare out at the Foothills,
where my Woman in the Mountain
resides full-length supine
head through torso hips sex
thighs kneecaps shins to toe.

THEN MAN STEPS IN

Pikes gathering clouds
around itself today, a shroud,
while the Woman in the Mountain
paints her perfect make-up with melting
snow. Then man steps in in the pure unseen
wind, emptying a week's worth of trash in a dozen
green-colored trash bins, knowing full-well lengths
of paper will fly out & up the damned branches of bare
black locust in between Pikes, the Woman in the Mountain,
& me.

BALANCE OF ANY MAN OR WOMAN

From the moment that black sky opens
to shed the first stars & planets
horizon flashes
its long spontaneous wink of red
in between
when I might spot
a huge hawk
on muddy path wondering
just what kind of bird it is before taking flight
to the tallest branch
of the nearest tree
mark the date make love
look off in the distance to a mountain peak
as if it were the future
refusing to be known
catch sight of moon near
full on way to mailbox
with nothing but the usual
junk, or watch my own shadow
grow length & height of walls & ceilings projected
by cruel Klieg lights from prison
masquerading as just another apartment complex
across the way
it's true I do want it my way
but never without others
influencing the impact
accepting it with as much openness
& resistance as the balance
of any man or woman
can muster.

DOWN THE SAN JUAN RIVER ON THE SOLSTICE

Good friend writes from Durango
that he & three others plan to head
down the San Juan twenty-seven miles
from Bluff to Mexican Hat, Utah, this
coming Sunday with recent runoff
giving them enough water to float on.

Anasazi clay shards & petroglyphs
                              follow
every move guiding
                generous spirits.

The lower stretch runs
        tandem kayaks through
                      a series of goosenecks
where the river practically snakes
                      back
in on itself.

He asked about how things are here.

                Coincidentally inquiring
about the International Ferry Terminal
                    from which he once embarked
on a journey
        as far north as St. John's, Newfoundland.

Just so happens
        we walked down there
                the day before

seeking info,
    & contradicting my earlier vow
                          not to battle
on foot all the heavy industry
      down that end of Commercial Street.

That small
      coincidence
           seemed to connect me
to him,
      maybe cross his mind at some point on the river
                                  or along the bank,
if they're allowed
      at all
           to get out & walk along that sacred ground.

Last night when the Scotia Prince
           pulled out of the terminal
exactly on time,
       8:00, fog
rolled in
      so thick even that huge ship was invisible,

& the only evidence
          it was out there was the Timetable
                         I've already got down
pat,
      & its fog horn sounding at
            the same nautical rate
                  the vessel itself would
on a clear night.

YOU HAVE TO TURN THE MAP AROUND

for **Anamika Bandopadhyay**

Four abodes in a year is enough to thank stars
more than four times over what with all
the bad roads in between.

The West was no less than its reputation
going in ahead of time, rough, vast,
dizzyingly so in that latter expanse.

I don't miss it all that much, but keep a map
of Colorado near me here in Maine,
a third its size out there, as mere

reminder of a chance to explore the territory.
From Denver & Boulder to that point at Eagle
you have to turn the map around just to get to Gypsum.

I fell in love with Glenwood Springs desiring
not to leave. Heavy wool blanket purchased there
on my 70th birthday swaddles us back to the hot springs,

or the bed on the top floor of the hotel.
No, we never made it to Silt, Rifle,
nor Parachute, didn't need to.

I know a woman with an utterly magical aura there
in Utah. Saw the Garden of the Gods, & lived
a block over from Kerouac's $1,000 shack.

LONG ENOUGH THERE TO GET HERE

It's not that
we lived in
the desert,
but hid out
long enough
there to
know our
bearings.

Far enough
away from
constant neon.
Near cactus
in the oasis.
The damn
damned up
carp below.

Coffee refills
free & so
were we
to traverse
the mountains,
even canyon
roads West.
Flagstaff.

Pikes Peak
in Colorado
Springs won't
budge from
memory, nor
Red Rocks &
Garden of
the Gods,

which is Good,
& called up
either at will
or unwillingly
real cowboys
herding cattle
in Greenland,
Colorado.

Long enough
in the desert
to get bearings.
Slept next cacti
in the oasis
dreaming
ahead to
this day.

AGAINST THE PROPENSITY

Against the propensity,
  propulsion at my age toward
    mere memory,
I continue to persist,
  insist on the clarity of the instant,
    carnality
of the Soul
  to the extent that even
    in dreams another man
will emerge
  saying he'd spent the night
    in the shelter of a coal mine,
& that for him
  death is nothing,
    but another destination.

THE IRASCIBLE, ORACULAR VOICE
OF EDWARD DORN

I never had to worry about success
Coming from where I came from
You were a success the minute you left town
   —**Edward Dorn, Success?**

DORN GOT AROUND. The hard way. He was intrepid: Villa Grove, Santa Fe, Gloucester, Pocatello, Seattle, Lawrence, all over, Mexico City, Colchester, Oxford, Denver, Boulder, the Languedoc, etc. Brought up a nomad, "I've fought for migration."[1] This inability to settle down, the vagrancy in a way, lends itself, out from those primitive bones, the quick-tempered, testy, irascible, edgy, oracular, almost scatting in a musical sense, rhythm to his voice, either in person, in interviews, or consistently shot down on paper. Analyzing the connection, he famously admitted to Stephen Fredman, "In other words, I find I'm always road-testing the language for a particular form of speech."[2]

The road, inextricable from Dorn's corporeal perceptions, abstract apprehensions. He'll draw beautiful & brutal conclusions. The poet sensed through trekking & reading, Carl Sauer, in particular, something beyond an aesthetic, rather, "Superior to an aesthetic…because it was like handling the bones of America."[3] The archaeological aspect taken directly back to Olson prior to Sauer. He'll transpose this digging of the geographic over to the textual by equating that physical ground, where in imaging the place of a poem, where one might never have been, but imagined, one begins "treating it as if it's a trowel into the archives so the past sheds a very different kind of light on the text."[4]

It's Olson early on impressed upon the young poet the notion of crossing boundaries (those imagined, or actual as barbed wire), getting to the other side, citing that of Rimbaud's despair, Poe's inverted jacket drunk on Fordham Road, or of course, the West itself: "TO GET TO THE OTHER SIDE," IS THE ONLY MORAL ACT THAT CAN POSSIBLY CORRECT THE WEST, AS EITHER GREEK OR U.S."[5] From there, he added that method/process equals to move,[6] proof also that, "since to move" as we get from O'Hara,[7] "is to love". In a letter recently acquired from Colchester, UK, written in 1966, (a year after documenting Native Americans in the Southwest while traversing Kerouac's famed Elko, via Pyramid, Battle Mountain, even Reno), answering an invitation to give a reading at Indiana University, becomes iconic of his long-running, life-long itinerant status, "…I have now no notion which I shall do or where be on our return next summer to the U.S."[8]

Antidote to his waywardness, to trepidation of no permanent home, other than boots of a wayfarer on solid ground, is that of immanence, or core of being set against, & within the world. An example of which occurred during the interim between researching / experiencing *The Shoshoneans* & Colchester's Fulbright, at the Berkeley Poetry Conference, where the day after Olson's reading he & Dorn revisited the conference event. Olson draws upon that constant, the *unknown*, pulled out of Dorn's story "C.B. & Q" in which a railroad man, gandy dancer, makes his way all the way from St. Joe's, Minnesota back down to New Mexico along the tracks, & that what arose was "a great unknown." He refers to it for both Dorn & himself as the "geological."[9] That earth under soles of boots of the wanderer as his only home. Dorn counters with what he learned from a Northern Paiute in what he first thought was Pyramid, NV, but suddenly recalled it was in Duck Valley that he heard the chant of the old Native American, "a death chant."[10] The young poet learns from the sound that pierces him to the core (what could be more immanent?), that it was a sound without referent without interpretation on any cultural level. So here, in love & friendship older & younger poet meet at "the literal, that attention" taking directly from the "chant does that thing… which is that the song lying in the thing itself is the only real… is something that goes right through everything…"[11] Much like Olson's dream Elephant in his book *West*:

>"…the Elephant altogether puzzling
>to me how we did go between trees through
>everything as a will passed through any obstacle…"[12]

Or a gandy dancer, poet, moving through the imminent & constant unknown via geology of earth, Minnesota to New Mexico.

>"Today: movement at any cost."[13]
>"The gain: to have a third term, that movement, or action,
>   is home."[14]

In a late interview, Matthew Cooperman attempts to draw the poet out on the subject of geography via Sauer's famous statement that, "The thing to be known is the landscape itself. It's known through the totality of its forms,"[15] expanding the series' questioning to ask whether Dorn's "work from very early on is what I would call a poetics of movement or lateralness, a discursivity that has to do with landscape."[16] & on to "I'm interested in whether you would consider yourself, among other things, a landscape poet to the degree that place becomes a character in certain poems like 'West of Moab,' 'Idaho Out,' *Gunslinger*."[17] In the interview, eventually, Dorn claims, "Landscape is not a poetic device. It's a material thing…If you are on earth you are on landscape, and there's nothing much you can do about that."[18] Both statements taken together encompass the distinction Sauer makes between landscape taken as it is with Space defining its morphology, & that cultural morphology after man's introduction into it, "…man expressing his place in nature as a distinct agent of modification."[19]

In his biography of Dorn, Tom Clark cites Sauer in relation to the poet's origin in Villa Grove, "…Carl Sauer, who had said of the historical ecology of the Illinois prairie, 'there is no stage of extractive or exhaustive cultivation…'"[20] Sauer goes further in his 1916 essay, *Pioneer Life in the Upper Illinois Valley*: "the open prairie was to be avoided, and many thought it must always remain a wasteland"; "One of the early superstitions held that the prairie was a desert, unable to support any vegetation other than native grasses…"; "…the winter climate of the prairies [is] too severe for human habitation."[21] Yet, Clark rightfully credits this very land as cause & influence on making Dorn the great tragic poet that he is by citing just two poems in which the morphology of the landscape by itself is slowly transmogrified into the ground the poet moves upon:

If Somebody Asks You Where You Come From Remember

There are two categories of soil
The soil of transport[a]
And the other is the soil of disintegration
Which can be found anywhere
but especially in the mountains.
Runoff goeth down to the valley,
into the soil of transport.

a. And that would be anywhere between the Appalachians and the Rockies.[22]

Clark goes on to use a second poem in Dorn's arsenal as proof of his uniqueness as a man able to dig up & out of what was believed by most as the fallow ground of the prairie, surrounding Villa Grove, a hard-won language like no other:

The Stripping of the River

The continental tree supports the margins
in return for involuntary atrophos
Which can now be called the Shale Contract
Not only are the obvious labors
In metal and grain and fuel extracted
But the spiritual genius is so apt
To be cloven from this plain of our green heart
And to migrate to the neutralized
And individualizing conditions of the coast
That this center of our true richness
Also goes there to aberrant rest
Bought by the silver of sunrise
And the gold of sunset.[23]

Of this "continental tree" Clark writes, "- i.e., his native Mid-western country, and all that was good of the human nature in it - may have been finally 'cloven from this plain,' enfeebled and wasted away by successive waves of diaspora, each bearing its promise of a pot of gold at the end of the prairie horizon as well as its potential for national and private loss."[24]

※

SAUER'S LANDSCAPE MORPHOLOGY defined by space is impurely extinguished as Dorn returns as passenger in a car driven by his younger sister 15 years after escaping. No land left other than what man has impinged upon in various cruel & deleterious ways. Willows removed by the river, now dirty, & the new homes now merely small scabs. There's a beautiful distinction he makes in recollection of receiving his eighth-grade diploma at a church outside Villa Grove in a place they drive through called Camargo, where because there is no vibration remaining of that experience, there is no feeling left, rather reduced to mere memory. Dorn, with high intellect wrenched out of the pain of this upbringing, "Our poverty was public…sold hot [stolen] corn for $2.50 a bushel during the second war…"[25] will not be limited to concrete dimensions of this place, but will inevitably in most all of his work lift it to declarative abstract heights. During this plains excursion the conflict between inherited "unconscious mimesis" recognized as handed down from his mother, & against what was her main source of information, TV, somehow gets temporarily ameliorated by, "Buying a new television for my people…,"[26] whereupon what comes on NET, a documentary of famine in India, gets elevated to a contrast between the sacred cow in that poor country & "no shortage of beef in this part of the country.":

> This is my place, but not my time. Any place can be mine. Time is irrelevant. So the place is simply once again, now. Time after all, plants its seed in the place.[27]

Sauer's notational rumor of the existence of prairie grasses only, replaced by a future transmitted through antenna & screen. Yet this tag-along drive across the prairie home becomes no longer about the geography of his birth, but the pure products of it: the twice drive-by on the main drag of his high school years recognizing Bobbie, a cripple who'd married one of the rich girls with pool table upstairs in an exceptional house, who'd attended an expensive, second rate school, recognized Dorn & moved toward him in his "terrible durability," while the poet turns away suddenly reminiscing, as if this time there were indeed vibrations remaining, about that *other* girl, who couldn't love, or make love to him, both crippled in their own way by the war, milieu, & mores, he is thankful now to have gotten past, with the caveat that could they have loved there in what was then Villa Grove she would not have chosen the public accountant, security, nor had a deformed child of her own.[28]

※

IT MAY BE no mean coincidence that in the massive *Collected Poems* published in Manchester, UK, thirteen years after the poet's death, the first poem, "Grasses", has the line:

"in our broken minds the counterplay"[29]

revealing that young Mr. Dorn is well aware of the wound lifted out of Illinois, made positive by discordances. It's this angle, & view, which distinguishes him from every other writer I've encountered, & in the fierce obliquity, dagger or bullet, erupts the blood beauty. The beauty of the angle & view is that it is always sharp, never blunted, subtle often times, but this fighter never pulls punches. In terms of the political, Donald Wesling refers to "the pronunciemento side of Dorn's mind, consciously quixotic kicks against the pricks..."[30] I'm not about to bother jotting down anything resembling his enemies list here. But I am drawn to that irascible quality of the man's character that eventually reaches full, obvious height in his book against the excesses of the '80s, *Abhorrences*.

No sense, however, leaping that far ahead already, there are lovely instances of cruel turns of phrase early on, even in his *Love Songs*, which I was most enamored of back then, even more so than most poems in *Geography & North Atlantic Turbine* (among the exceptions, "From Gloucester Out", of course, where I lived at the time), when I met him that afternoon circa 1978 up at Goddard College in Richard Grossinger's kitchen, Creeley head-down on the table, Dorn hovering above him, protective. When I asked if he knew the work of Sidney Goldfarb the whole room ignited with Dorn's enthusiasm over the young man & his work, even mentioning Peabody, MA, where Sidney was born, grew up, & fought his way out all the way to Boulder, founding the Creative Writing Department at the University of Colorado, where he & Ed would teach & become friends. No, no need to leap into the future to find Dorn's irascibility, when right there in his 1975 quite premature *Collected* (or Harvey Brown's 1969 & 1970 Frontier Press chapbooks), one could find:

>   when I unsheathe
> a word of wrong temper
> it is to test that steel
> across the plain between us.[31]

※

>   -look
> I insist on my voice...

> if you were my own time's possession
> I'd tell you to fuck off
> with such penetration
> you'd never stop gasping
> and pleasure unflawed
> would light up our lives, pleasure
> unrung by the secretly expected
> fingers of last sunday…[32]

In *The Lost America of Love*, Sherman Paul's book of essays on Creeley, Dorn, & Duncan, the author writes, "You don't mess with Dorn; he knows the score, and what is more, as everyone from the beginning of his career remarks on as memorable virtue, he has figured it for himself."[33] Paul will revisit (as I have above) the lost love Dorn alludes to in "Driving across the Prairie" back in Villa Grove, "We needed love. We couldn't have it."[34] He'll cite the poet's love beyond women:

> An occasional woman, won't
> though I wish she could,
> justify a continent [35]

to children in "The Common Lot":

> A masterful forbearance, the children
> too, playing on the sidewalk,
>
> and in the vacant lot, that
> they all don't go away, one by one,
>
> one could love them both, the trees
> and the children.
>
>   … My daughter alone
>
> on the mound of rubbish sand disappears
> into a cave of pink rug.
> …
> Ah. The vacant lot is vast, I can speak of love
> only at the edge. [36]

& famously, for those who know the work, of men:

> Pure existence, even in the crowds
> I love
> will never be possible for me
>
> even with the men I love
>   This is
> the guilt
> that kills me
>   My adulterated presence
>
> but please believe with all men
> I love to be [37]

From one of Dorn's homages to his mentor Charles Olson, here Sherman Paul, one of the first scholars to address Olson's oeuvre in depth, Olson's Push, 1978, masterfully prefaces Dorn's poem with the poet's own critical take on the The Maximus Poems to reveal the kind of toughness his language exhibits, whether on love, or power in the world at large:

> I don't trust the universe. I would kick it in the teeth if it came near me. Because I have thus far seen the universe to be in the hands of such men...[38]

Love, land, anger, & the oracular thrust of his future politics come together all in one fairly long poem gathered early on in the 1965 collection *Geography* dedicated to Olson, titled, "The Sense Comes Over Me, and the Waning Light of Man by the 1st National Bank" in which he dares first introduce the character of his stepfather,

> My stepfather stood on the corner
> by the national bank, quiet...[39]

the same man whom Clark in the second chapter of his biography points out as Glen Abercrombie "revealing a severe side to his own temper, rewarded the boy's obstreperous displays with whippings."[40] Just one source to the wounds that make a poet speak. I don't know why a few hours ago as I reread these pages of Dorn's the word lapidary welled up from some place inside me here in Denver = stonecutter, engraver, gemstone polisher, applied to Dorn's lines, his mind, attention?

> I became the land and wandered out of it.
> Sharp...[41]

Sharp as a diamond, but also a tack, as the writer will use his tools of language to attempt the escape from,

> that ceaseless speculation over
> the ways of love
> into the darker borders
> of my wounded middle years,
>   a practical self-pity
>   There was a girl
>   who was a resolution
>   with whom I walked the empty streets
>   and climbed the watertower for one night
>   to show myself, she standing a white spot of summer
>   on the ground, and looked out I did
>   over the lights of a realm I thought grander than
>   and any of it, altogether, was very little, and when
>   the pictographic scratches in the silver paint told me
>   as I walked around
>   the cat-walk expression of what happened in the 1930's
>   men vomiting from hunger
>   on the thin sidewalk below, a lonely mason
>   with his business ring on, but beyond,
>   in the little shoe repair shops the men,
>   part of a hopeless vigilante, exhaling the slow mustard gas
>   of World War I. My mother, moving slowly in the grim kitchen
>   and my stepfather moving slowly down the green rows of corn
>   these are my unruined and damned hieroglyphs.
>   Because they form
> the message of men stooping down
> in my native land, and father an entire conglomerate
> of need and wasted vision...[42]

He damn-well got that out of his system, alright!! But there's more that sticks in his craw. He's up & outed the traumatic causes of his own & others' suffering in this land of unplenty, the War to end all wars, & results of stockmarket crash, then again, there's the continuing bullshit of a Johnson taking over for an assassinated Kennedy, the poet's condemnation of his own "gutless generation," while "nineteen year olds / invaded the white house today, a screen / was put up to shield the nervous exit / of Ladybird, they sang and refused to move, / she split…"

His rant against America is still far from done in this masterful opus. He'll share with the reader that that protest by young people there in DC allowed him to "be a less schizophrenic american, a little of the pus was spooned out of my brain, I gave / an arbitrary grade to a backward black girl / I remembered to spit on the sidewalk / when I thought of the first 35 hundred marines / who landed in Vietnam yesterday…"

No, not done by a longshot, Dorn goes from being irascible about the past & present to oracular, foreshadowing what we have now a full half century ahead, "I warn you world of good intention the birth of Mohammed / will be fought in this neck of the cut-off world / devoid of the culture that spawned it consciously / and moved on, any new blood will / turn to an unnumberable plasma / we could still walk into the banks / and demand the money…"[43]

※

DORN WROTE THAT he read spontaneously. If so, must have written that way, too. The two go hand in hand. He believed gods were "spontaneous men who appear on earth."[44] In his fine book, *The Culture of Spontaneity: Improvisation and the Arts in Postwar America*, Daniel Belgrad, examining the work across the board by such artists, writers, musicians, dancers, philosophers as Kline, Krasner, Rauschenberg, Kerouac, Olson, Williams, Coltrane, Monk, Parker, Cunningham, Jung, etc., the author quotes Dorn writing to Olson regarding his "Projective Verse" essay, "You say it I think in all that about field, and by the way I like the nice clear way you put it ie. 'that the choice of word or particle will be spontaneous' which it is."[45] Belgrad records an even earlier episode, when in 1956 Dorn wrote to Olson from San Francisco that Creeley had brought round, "another writer, Jack Kerouac, who is a great man, I am sure (I read some note-statements of his on prose that were as much to say how you do it if you want with no bullshit." Olson responded, "This guy Kerouac sounds good. How about getting me a copy of this thing you speak of, to see?"[46] Of course, these notes on prose were famously hung upon a wall above Ginsberg's desk when he wrote *Howl*: "Belief & Technique for Modern Prose: List of Essentials" & "Essentials of Spontaneous Prose":

1. Scribbled secret notebooks and wild typewritten pages,
   for yr own joy…
5. Something that you feel will find its own form
6. Be crazy dumbsaint of the mind
7. Blow as deep as you want to blow
8. Write what you want bottomless from bottom of the mind…
10. No time for poetry but exactly what is…
28. Composing wild, undisciplined, pure, coming in from
    under, crazier the better…[47]

※

PROCEDURE. Time being of the essence in the purity of speech, sketching language is undisturbed flow from the mind of personal secret idea-words, blowing (as per jazz musician) on subject of image.

METHOD. No periods separating sentence-structures already arbitrary riddled by false colons and timid usually needless commas – but the vigorous space dash separating rhetorical breathing (as jazz musician drawing breath between outblown phrases) – 'measured pauses which are the essentials of our speech' – 'divisions of the sounds we hear' – 'time and how to note it down.' (William Carlos Williams)

CENTER OF INTEREST. Begin not from preconceived idea of what to say about image but from jewel center of interest in subject of image at moment of writing, and write outwards swimming in sea of language to peripheral release and exhaustion – … – tap from yourself, blow! – now! – your way is your only way – 'good' – or 'bad' – always honest, ('ludicrous'), spontaneous, 'confessional,' interesting, because not 'crafted.' Craft is craft.[48]

※

Extremely influential documents. Ginsberg didn't refer to them exactly in his "Notes for Howl..." but they're there:

> By 1955 I wrote poetry adapted from prose seeds, journals, scratchings, arranged by phrasing or breath groups into little short-line patterns according to ideas of measure of American speech I'd picked up from W. C. Williams' imagist preoccupations...I thought I wouldn't write a poem, but just write what I wanted to without fear, let my imagination go, open secrecy, and scribble magic lines from my real mind — sum up my life — something I wouldn't be able to show anybody, write for my own soul's ear...long saxophone-like chorus lines I knew Kerouac would hear the sound of – taking off from his own inspired prose line really a new poetry.[49]

※

THREE YEARS AFTER Dorn, privy to Kerouac's note-statements of prose, who solicits work from him, but none other than LeRoi Jones in New York City hanging out with Ornette Coleman, Archie Shepp, Don Cherry, Roy Haynes, Cecil Taylor, etc., (talk about jazz musicians drawing breath between outblown phrases!!). Jones caught sight of Dorn's work in little magazines like *Ark II, Evergreen Review, Measure, Migrant, Moby I, & no less*, on the desk of Donald Allen, while the Grove editor contemplated including a sheaf for his forthcoming, earth-shaking anthology. Jones asked Dorn to consider sharing poems for his own small mag at the time, *Yugen*, a concept in traditional Japanese aesthetics: *profound, mysterious sense of the beauty of the universe & the sad beauty of human suffering.*

That was 1959. Within a year what beauty Jones saw in Dorn's work, both mysterious & sad, got a chance to be collected into Ed's first book with the help of Elsa Dorfman, then a secretary at Grove Press, calling herself, "The Paterson Society," & offering to subsidize *The Newly Fallen* under the auspices of LeRoi's Totem Press. It's still only among the first few letters exchanged between the two poets, but here September 29, 1960, listen to the innate jazz rush in the breath of Jones advocating that Dorn take advantage of the creative philanthropy come his way:

> This has to be quick because you need a book now rather than single shots, &c. Well, only reason I lagged jumping at it was lack of lucre, &c. Now, Elsa Dorfman's "Paterson Society" has agreed to put up bread for about a 40 some odd page book...which we're supposed to have OUT by the time you reach disyear town. 20 FEB. (I know whew! Many expletives!
>
> But I say I'm game to jam it together & work furious with printers &c. If you are & you can get some kind of MSS to me...BUT...mss will have to be in my hands by 17 DECEMBER, or I can't see how in hell it'll make it. I know it's fast &c. But Ellie just let me hear today, this morning & I'm quick to get it off to you so I don't pull no leadfoot act on this end... I've gotta hear quick (queek). SO?
>
> Fast, LeRoi[50]

Here, again, Dorn was listening to the Village beat of a different drummer, while the work Jones & Dorfman loved in Ed's voice was at that time quite the opposite: rural, elegiac, modulated, even classical ("My desire is to be / a classical poet")[51] as Olson immediately referred to his first collections as, "Klessick."[52] However, Jones's influence in the already brief correspondence is evident, when eight letters later, after traveling to New York for a reading, & meeting LeRoi & his wife Hettie for the first time, Dorn returns to Santa Fe, & writes back:

> Brought back from said apple two delicious [Sonny] Rollins, the one with Limehouse Blues & Doxie on it w/ Teddy Edwards on back, you know...Wow. We live in two different worlds. And my ideal. Jesus. B quick, B lovely, B with it. Actually Rollins was the first man in space.[53]

✻

JONES'S INFLUENCE ON Dorn across space & time cannot be underestimated. Sure, they argued about the political situation at that time, what with Jones, part of a delegation sponsored by the Pro-Castro, Fair-Play for Cuba Committee heading down in 1960 to observe just how the revolution fared; a couple years later the Cuban Missile Crisis, etc., but they hung tough in their correspondence. Despite differences, they were equally radical in their views, if not approaches. Just six months after Ed's joy about the jazz he brought home from the reading & visit to LeRoi in NYC, he alludes to the importance of the visit, but this time waxes political all the way from Pocatello, Idaho:

> I get so fucking lonely here, I'd like to tell you this: In NY last spring I thot you the only man who said anything, stood for anything, anything AND STILL DO... Poets are the only fucking people I can stand in this era, everybody else is not with it... Frankly when I got that blurb from the Cuva committee w/ Elaine DeKooning etc, I was so fucking embarrassed I didn't know whether to sign it or not... poets are that only outcast force that cannot gain by being chided with plumbing...None of us can help it that this is a sick time.[54]

Twenty-nine years later John Wright, in an interview with Dorn at his home in Boulder, refers to a letter to LeRoi Jones he'd dug up in the archives at UCLA, written exactly a year & a week after the one just cited above, in which Dorn refers to himself as an "anti state cat."[55] Wright is using the recently published, highly charged, & political book, *Abhorrences*, (which flayed the obese decade of the 80s), as a tract that could possibly label the poet as Marxist or anarchist. In what for me is this wonderful angle Edward Dorn takes by being apolitical in order to become simply against everything:

> One of my problems is that I don't really have any politics because I could never really understand what an anarchist was. ...I think that the state is the most pernicious invention,...that man ever perfected... I guess I'm not an anarchist. Actually, I'm not anything, really; I'm just against everything because I know it's bad... Which is not a politics, actually.[56]

I believe Dorn's & Jones's poetics equally radical. The former's apolitical stance in his writing, substituting an all out "Fuck 'em all"[57] attitude, is as broad a swipe possible of resistance, which situates the protest in the writing & Soul of the poet, contrasts with the latter's need for the poem to be one of action, exemplified by Baraka's Keynote Address at the 2008 Ed Dorn Symposium at the University of Colorado, Boulder, regarding the early distinction, also evident in their early correspondence:

> But as I moved more directly into political activism and away from

the icy literary world, I grew impatient with a mere infatuation with language. That language that I still admired was to signify action, a move away from the given, the static, the dead.[58]

I remember, vividly, four years earlier in February of 2004 infiltrating Baraka's large entourage at the reception upstairs from the auditorium at Mass College of Art (believing poets can't trespass) in order to hand him a signed copy of my own, *The Book of Assassinations*, title of which I believed summed up the most crucially determining factor of politics to that point in time in America, if not world at large. Amidst sidelong glances of disdain from his people at the white guy with the book, while he sat on the edge of a table, dour, sullen, no one speaking to him, Amiri lifted his head, smiled a smile of recognition first at the image of Nadar's photo of Baudelaire, "Ah, Baudelaire!", & then, I can only imagine, his further acknowledgment of the title, perhaps reminding him of his 1965 poem "Black Art":

> ...we want "poems that kill."
> Assassin poems, Poems that shoot
> guns. [59]

After all, what I recorded in my notes from his lecture just delivered to the full-house audience downstairs in the auditorium, finds Baraka fuming:

> that one tenth of one percent of people run everything in this country, acknowledging our backward president as one of those corporate killers, ne'er-do-wells in youth spreading their seed all round rising to positions of oppression, (the audience could all feel it, this rant against all those who feel a moral obligation to be against other peoples' pleasure, the culture or absence of it most think comes from TV), inventing the low coup opposing it to the Japanese haiku, knowing most of the world is not white, & that the direction of the world will be decided by them, (which must have been news to someone, I guess), laughing, that blowing whitey to hell may not be such a bad idea, (but hey, he's here too, with some of his own people), reminding us that it was not by choice, but by terror, the slave ship pictured in his play *The Slave*, written when he was still known as Jones, Baraka calling for the young students in the audience to, "Read read read! You may never get a chance again, you women gonna get pregnant, you guys

jobs for the mon, & come home exhausted fall on the bed asleep, what you think you gonna read Aristotle? Publish yourself, go to Kinko's, make a Kinko's book out of what you believe, distribute them around yourselves. Be creative! What you going to produce other than expensive feces? Study now!" Then a grand poem about his grandmother where he conjectures that if the people of his race can figure out why their grandmothers were always humming, he hums it, sings it, raps it, drums it, & plumbs the answer, as if it were the *Aum* of the sound of the Universe, the hum goes on as a kind of preverbal choric chant like the Gregorian records he ordered as a librarian in Puerto Rico in the service because he & the other servicemen didn't know what they were, but wanted to, along with the twenty volumes of Kafka because they didn't know him, but wanted to, & the grandmothers hum as antennae as radar for what they knows comes eventually inevitably as trouble & the devil the rent bill & the man & Baraka lifts that tone up to around some pitch he learned from Miles or Coltrane when he mused on liner notes for the latter's album in 1964, *Live at Birdland: One of the most baffling things about America is that despite its essentially vile profile, so much beauty continues to exist here*, tearing that tone up out of the crib where rats threaten at night filled with anguish a pain inherited before birth we whites don't ever get lifting it way up past stars past death that realm of infinity where horses of the apocalypse are colorless.[60]

In his Keynote back in Boulder in 2008 with the country on the brink of economic collapse, he said, "We need Dorn right now…What we miss in Dorn is an actual gladiator poet at the very top of the number. We had fought against fools and liars all our poetic lives…We must not only talk about Dorn we must read him."[61]

Let's read then. Randomly *here*. In depth in the future. These 10 tracts, which I've sought out intuitively, quite spontaneously in pages of volumes surrounding me, volumes I suspected might like gold in a fairly well-known Colorado stream pan out, while thousands of other examples could have proven just as useful, let this gladiator speak:

※

Where are the Barbarians at the gate now that we need them to dismember and lay waste this decadent power?[62]

Chief George the Supercilious quaffed a horn of Houstonian proportions and punched a Greek in the head and swaggered to his feet, a huge oath on his lips which could be read from the farthest reaches of the vast Hall - WENCHE!! "A horn of QuayleAle for the rePUBlican Warlord!"[63]

> I'm going to take this fucking year
> For which I've been waiting a long time
> And I am going to rip it from its sappy
> Stupid throat to its overfermented balls
> And then I'm going to wrap its toxic guts
> Around the first sports announcer I hear. [64]

> I've always found much
> to recommend
> in the slogan "Soak the Rich"
> but I've never found
> much discussion regarding
> the uses of that marinade.
> I have one other modest proposal:
> feed them to the poor. [65]

If you're talking about the Dutch... It's not like everybody's two paychecks away from homelessness, which is what they say here. Two paychecks away. I think that's optimistic. I think it's a paycheck and a half![66]

> Out of the Sunset movement
> Out of the Sunrise invasion [67]

> 29 Pay Attention he screams then bites um
>   And spits minute words in ums ears
>   Very small words in ums ears
>   This is no **hypothetical radical** sweetheart
>   This is a **systematic arrangement** like salt. [68]

Sanders is the medicine man of our era. He looks like the man who could have shot Lincoln but didn't. All the fabulous force of his shamanism is thrown into the "total assault on the culture." A true Fugstar. The first hero we've had who could stand up to all those russian chinese examples. But peace is real too.[69]

> Kicking Ed Meese
> is like kicking a toadstool.
> No "my fellow citizens"
> Ed Meese is not the problem.
> The stoolies on Capitol Hill
> want this loyal fan of the police
> for Attorney General so desperately
> acceptance would be hard to hide.
> What's this talk of tradition?
> This is the tradition. [70]

A time capsule which when broken open will reveal the man inside turned into the name his chums called him from the simple frustration of being unable to think of something else. New York. Or you can forget the debt and call it Boston. I can't quite deal with the man who remembers to speak my name alongside a load of other matter about me he's trying hard to forget. A white man, any man who makes himself white discovers spirit he covers himself with ashes of the blowing sign of the universe, local materials.[71]

This last an example of the irascible & oracular, hand in hand. In the *Chicago Review* special issue, *Edward Dorn: American Heretic*, Keith Tuma draws to a close his "Late Dorn" essay with this more than prescient prediction for disaster by the poet:

> [T]he nonempowered just try to get on with their jihads...Hijack a Concorde with a kitchen-knife would be the ultimate low-tech solution. So it is, so it increaseth.[72]

Here, also, speaking of a wildly oracular world view the quote by the reviewer of Dorn's massive *Collected Poems* from Carcanet in the *World Socialist Website* of all places:

This is from Dorn's very last interview in 1999: "Where the next war will be, of the Kosovo kind, we don't really know. It could be the sources of the Tigris and the Euphrates because the Kurds are a lot more numerous than anybody else who is in that situation. They're surrounded by enemies because they've got the Syrians and the Turks and the Iraqis. And, to one extent or another, the Iranians a little bit off that. We're talking about the prime conditions for creating everlasting powerful, intense and intensified enemies." Talk about poets as the "antennae of the race."[73]

※

CAN'T QUITE BRING myself to end right there. Rather, suddenly recall chaos swirled around me at the ArcheTime Conference in NYC in 2008 held at a former X-rated movie theater, Director Olga interrupting each participant as to when their five minutes were up. Come my turn, changed the scene from floor to stage, rather than just stand there at the end of the aisle ushers used to roam with flashlights, from newly propped chair & table, announced, "I'm going to try to shove the tail into the mouth of the snake of Time, & read what I planned last, first." Here then, returning to the initial Fredman/Dorn interview, Shaman in his own right, Dorn, gathers ritual tools, cruel truths, love & compassion, hard-won poetic skills, to take the floor, the stage, & have the last word:

> There are certain Obligations of the Divine, whether those can be met or not. Part of the function is to be alert to Spirit, and not so much write poetry as to compose the poetry that's constantly written on the air. What I've read and what I hear merge to make the field in which I compose…There must be something in "being a poet," and it's demonstrably not material, so I therefore suspect it must be divine. The obligations would be self-evident. It's divining like science is divining…The conception is sheer poetry…[74]

*   *   *   *   *

ADDENDUM: The same day Michael Boughn in Toronto, Editor of *Dispatches from the Poetry Wars*, shared a photo of eight men laughing uproariously, including Reagan, Meese, & Bush I, I happened on a stray recollection from a former student of Dorn's in Boulder, which reveals to a degree, further than even previously imagined, his teacher's prescient, oracular take on a decade ahead of time, which would eventually become his irascible, political masterpiece of the period, *Abhorrences*:

> On my first night in the graduate poetry workshop with Edward Dorn at the University of Colorado, Ed began his weekly rant with the phrase "looking back on the eighties" — and followed it up with a cynical, but deadly accurate account of the writing that was on the Republican wall. The year was 1981. I marveled, in my innocence, at the moxie of one who would feign to know the contents of a decade that had only just begun, but I also became fatally attracted to the vigor of it, the nerve, focused in laser-like concentration on the Gipper and his ilk. To me, Ed was like one of the wrathful deities of Tibetan Buddhism: outwardly wrapped in robes of incinerating fire, but inwardly possessed of a core of compassion and tenderness.[75]

References

[1] Edward Dorn, *Views*, Edited by Donald Allen (San Francisco: Four Seasons Foundation, 1980) 14.

[2] Stephen Fredman, *Roadtesting the Language: An Interview with Edward Dorn*, (San Diego: University of CA, 1978) 38.

[3] Edward Dorn, "An Interview with Barry Alpert," 1972, *Interviews*, Edited by Donald Allen (Bolinas: Four Seasons Foundation, 1980) 22.

[4] Edward Dorn, "Poetry Is a Difficult Labor: Last Lectures" 1999, *Ed Dorn Live*, (Ann Arbor: The University of Michigan Press, 2007) 127.

[5] Charles Olson, *A Bibliography on America for Ed Dorn*, (San Francisco: Four Seasons Foundation, 1965) 5.

[6] Ibid., 5.

[7] Frank O'Hara, "In Memory of My Feelings" *The Collected Poems of Frank O'Hara*, Edited by Donald Allen (New York: Knopf, 1979) 256.

[8] Edward Dorn, *Letter to Seamus Cooney*, English Dept. University of Indiana from Colchester, Essex, UK, June 19, 1966.

[9] Charles Olson, Edward Dorn, "Reading at Berkeley - The Day After" Edited by Ralph Maud in The Shoshoneans (Expanded Edition) (Albuquerque: University of New Mexico Press, 2013) 161.

[10] Ibid., 162.

[11] Ibid., 163.

[12] Charles Olson, *West* (London: The Golliard Press, 1966) [4].

[13] Charles Olson, PROPRIOCEPTION in *Additional Prose*, Edited by Donald Allen (Bolinas: Four Seasons Foundation, 1974) 17.

[14.] Ibid., 18.

[15.] Edward Dorn, "Waying the West: The Cooperman Interviews" in *Ed Dorn Live*, (Ann Arbor: The University of Michigan Press, 2007) 96.

[16.] Ibid., 97.

[17.] Ibid., 98.

[18.] Ibid., 99.

[19.] Carl Ortwin Sauer, "The Morphology of Landscape" in *Land & Life*, (Berkeley: U CA Press, 1963) 333.

[20.] Tom Clark, *Edward Dorn: A World of Difference*, (Berkeley: North Atlantic Books, 2002) 74.

[21.] Carl Ortwin Sauer, "Pioneer Life in the Upper Illinois Valley" in *Land & Life*, (Berkeley: UCA Press, 1963) 12.

[22.] Edward Dorn, *Collected Poems* (Manchester, UK: Carcanet, 2012) 629.

[23.] Ibid., 361.

[24.] Clark, 74.

[25.] Edward Dorn, "Driving Across the Prairie," in *Some Business Recently Transacted in the White World*, (West Newbury, MA: Frontier Press, 1971) 60, 63.

[26.] Grateful acknowledgment to Jennifer Dunbar Dorn for clarification of my earlier misreading of both Clark & poet's reminiscence by imagining him watching the program during adolescence: "It's in the present that he buys a TV for 'his people' his mother and stepfather. It's N.E.T. (educational tv channel) that has the program on famine in India (I was there and remember this)." email, January 21, 2017.

[27.] Dorn, "Driving…" 57.

28. Ibid., 64.

29. Edward Dorn, *Collected Poems,* (Manchester, UK: Carcanet, 2012) 5.

30. *Internal Resistances: The Poetry of Edward Dorn*, Edited by Donald Wesling (Berkeley: U of CA Press, 1985) 4.

31. Edward Dorn, *Twenty-four Love Songs*, (West Newbury, MA: Frontier Press, 1969) 3.

32. Ibid., 6.

33. Sherman Paul, *The Lost America of Love: Rereading Robert Creeley, Edward Dorn, and Robert Duncan*, (Baton Rouge: Louisiana State University Press, 1981) 78.

34. Ibid., 108.

35. Ibid., 104.

36. Edward Dorn, *The Newly Fallen*, (NY, NY: Totem Press, 1961) 27.

37. Edward Dorn, *From Gloucester Out*, (London: The Matrix Press, 1964) 2.

38. Paul. 99.

39. Edward Dorn, "The Sense Comes Over Me, and the Waning Light of Man by the 1st National Bank" in *Geography*, (London: Fulcrum Press, 1965) 66.

40. Clark, 55.

41. Edward Dorn, *Geography*, 68.

42. Ibid., 68.

43. Ibid., 69.

44. Edward Dorn, "What I See in The Maximus Poems" in *Views*, 40.

[45] Edward Dorn, Letter to Charles Olson, Feb 6, 1960 in Daniel Belgrad, *The Culture of Spontaneity: Improvisation and the Arts in Postwar America* (Chicago: U of Chicago Press, 1998) 123.

[46] Ibid., 200.

[47] Jack Kerouac, "Belief & Technique for Modern Prose: List of Essentials" in *New American Story*, Edited by Donald M. Allen & Robert Creeley (Harmondsworth, UK: Penguin, 1971) 276.

[48] Ibid., 277.

[49] Allen Ginsberg, "Notes for Howl and Other Poems," in *The Poetics of the New American Poetry*, Edited by Donald Allen & Warren Tallman (New York: Grove Press, 1973) 318.

[50] LeRoi Jones [Amiri Baraka] Letter to Edward Dorn in *Amiri Baraka & Edward Dorn: The Collected Letters*, Edited by Claudia Moreno Pisano (Albuquerque: U of New Mexico Press, 2013) 28.

[51] Edward Dorn, *Idaho Out* [dedicated: To Hettie and Roi] (London: Fulcrum Press, 1965) 6.

[52]. Clark, 393.

[53] *Letters*, March 13, 1961, 36.

[54] Ibid., October 21, 1961, 61.

[55] Ibid., October 27, 1962, 107.

[56] John Wright, "An Interview with Edward Dorn," *Chicago Review* Vol. 49, Is. 3/4 (Summer 2004) 194.

[57] Claudia Moreno Pisano, in *Baraka & Dorn Letters*, 25.

[58] Amiri Baraka, "Ed Dorn and the Western World" Preface to *Baraka & Dorn Letters*, xxiii.

59. LeRoi Jones, "Black Art," *Chicken Bones: A Journal for Literary & Artistic African American Themes*, http://www.nathanielturner.com/blackart.htm.

60. Robert Gibbons, "In the Words of Amiri Baraka at Mass College of Art, 2/25/04" in *Travels Inside the Archive* (Brownfield, ME: Edge of Maine Editions, 2009) 58.

61. Baraka, Preface to *Baraka & Dorn Letters*, xxiv.

62. Dorn, from "Languedoc Varorium: A Defense of Heresy & Heretics' in *Collected Poems* (Manchester, UK: Carcanet, 2012) 825.

63. Dorn, "The RePUBlicans" in *Way West* (Santa Rosa: Black Sparrow Press, 1993) 192.

64. Dorn, "Nineteen Eighty Eight Maniac" in *Abhorrences* (Santa Rosa: Black Sparrow, 1990) 136.

65. Dorn, "Recette Economique" in *Abhorrences* 45.

66. Dorn, John Wright, "Interview," *Chicago Review*, 207.

67. Dorn, [Untitled] in *Recollections of Gran Apachería* (San Francisco: Turtle Island, 1974) 32.

68. Dorn, "The I.D. Runs the Actual Furnishings" in *The Cycle* (West Newbury, MA: Frontier Press, 1971) [22].

69. Dorn, "The Outcasts of Foker Plat: News from the States" in *Views*, 82.

70. Dorn, "The Ed Meese Scrolls" in Abhorrences, 38.

71. Dorn, *Some Business Recently Transacted in the White World*, (West Newbury: Frontier, 1971) 81.

72. Keith Tuma, "Late Dorn," *Chicago Review* Vol. 49, Is. 3/4 (Summer 2004) 251.

73. Andras Gyorgy, "Ed Dorn and the Politics of the New American Poetry" *World*

Socialist Website, October 9, 2013. https://www.wsws.org/en/articles/2013/10/09/dorn-o09.html

[74.] Fredman, Interview, 8.

[75.] John Wolff, "Edward Dorn: An 80's Reminiscence" from *Cento Magazine*, Electronic Poetry Center, Buffalo http://epc.buffalo.edu/authors/dorn/DORN_CENTO/dorn_wolff.html

ALSO BY ROBERT GIBBONS

To Know Others, Various & Free
Traveling Companion
This Time
Jagged Timeline
Travels Inside the Archive
Beyond Time: New & Selected Work, 1977-2007
Body of Time
The Book of Assassinations
Streets for Two Dancers

The Degas
Olson/Still: Crossroad
Rhythm of Desire & Resistance
This Vanishing Architecture
Of DC
Lover, Is This Exile?
Ardors
The Woman in the Paragraph
Yellow & Black
Below California, Below This

Printed in the USA
CPSIA information can be obtained
at www.ICGtesting.com
JSHW021037170224
57553JS00005B/101